Representing Children's Book Characters

by
MARY E. WILSON

THE SCARECROW PRESS, INC.
Metuchen, N.J., & London 1989

Permission credits are listed in the Acknowledgments, pages vii and viii.

British Library Cataloguing-in-Publication data available.

Library of Congress Cataloging-in-Publication Data

Wilson, Mary E., 1935–
 Representing children's book characters / by Mary E. Wilson.
   p.   cm.
 Includes indexes.
 ISBN 0-8108-2169-9
 1. Children—Books and reading. 2. Children—Costume.
3. Characters and characteristics in literature. 4. Libraries, Children's—
Activity programs. 5. Children's literature—Study and teaching—Aids
and devices. I. Title.
Z1037.A1W645   1989
028.5—dc19   88-31286

Copyright © 1989 by Mary E. Wilson

Manufactured in the United States of America

Printed on acid-free paper ∞

PUBLISHER'S NOTE

THE SUGGESTIONS FOR dramatizations included in this book are intended for librarian or teacher use with students. If performances are planned for the public, even if presented by a library or school, permission must be obtained ahead of time from the copyright holder of the work being dramatized.

CONTENTS

	Acknowledgments	vii
I.	INTRODUCTION AND SUGGESTIONS FOR USING THIS BOOK	1
II.	CHOOSING A CHARACTER AND CAPTURING ITS ESSENCE	6
III.	PUTTING THE COSTUME TOGETHER	15
IV.	IDEAS FOR CHARACTERS FROM MOTHER GOOSE	38
V.	IDEAS FOR CHARACTERS FROM FABLES AND FOLK AND FAIRY TALES	42
VI.	IDEAS FOR CHARACTERS FROM PICTURE STORY BOOKS AND READERS	48
VII.	IDEAS FOR CHARACTERS FROM FICTION	69
VIII.	IDEAS FOR CHARACTERS FROM BIOGRAPHY	85
IX.	A FEW NOTES ON NON-FICTION	93
X.	WHAT TO DO WITH A COSTUMED BOOK CHARACTER; OR, PUTTING ON A CELEBRATION	95
XI.	IDEAS FOR A CLASS PRESENTATION OF A SINGLE TITLE	108
XII.	APPENDIXES	125
	A. Teacher and Parent Information Forms	125
	B. Parade Sign-Up Forms	131
	C. Scripts	136
	D. Book Celebration Programs	145
	E. Meanderings from Mary	148
	Subject Index	151
	Author/Title Index	156
	Character Name/Character Type Index	161

ACKNOWLEDGMENTS

To my mother for reading aloud from the world of Pooh and Piglet and Christopher Robin; to my father for using rich and complex language; to my brother for championing me. To Sylvia Ashton Warner, Harry the Dirty Dog, and the family for leading me from nursing to teaching. To Jeanette Veatch for responding to my journal writing. To Nina Martin for rescuing me from failure as a librarian. To Sidney, Sandy, and Laurie for enduring, with love, living with me.

To Dr. James Perry and the Chandler Unified School District for permitting description of Erie School activities. To Elsie Layland for being a genius at costuming and to René Wiley and Mary Murphy for following in her book character activities in the library. To Nancy Grubb for sharing her Clifford and much more, and to Carol Carlson and Carla Cantrell for using their considerable artistic talent for book celebrations. To Ann Wood for furnishing her script for the KXYZ-TV production and to Betty Wilson for sharing her monkey and cap patterns. To Mary Thielen for giving good advice. To Airi Riikonen and Janice Sherick for providing details about book character activities at their schools. And to Reed Ethington, Bud Wood, and Maria Worth and the following current and past Erie teachers for making time to celebrate books and for providing inspiration, ideas, and support:

Genny Appleton	Michelle Hamilton	Peggy Pillow
Sandy Bell	Julia Hardy	Delpha Price
Ruth Bosse	Barb Hartman	Joan Reinke
Chris Bozarth	Fonda Hodsden	Georgina Rico
Velma Buddemeyer	Diane Johnston	Karen Ross
Steve Bursi	Jan Langer	Joanne Sippel
Dotty Deschenes	Marianne McMurrin	John Slater
Edna Donovan	Betty Manning	Cheryl Smith
Cindy Dugan	John Melka	Georgi Weintraub
Cecelia DuPriest	Lee Meschino	Clyde Williams
Ginny Enright	Andrea Moyers	Pat Workman
Tony Fanucci	Rita Nuest	

To Erie parents, students, and especially Library Club members for keeping the book celebrations going for over 12 years with their great participation and response. To Mrs. Schaab's class for making the Dark Thing retreat and to Renee Smith and Mrs. Hodsden's class for presenting "The Wish Giver." To Marcy Thomas for reporting on the book parade in the *Erie Express*, to Lynda Barney for illustrating Marcy's article, and to Brian Marquez, Emory Huffines, and Stephanie Spraggins for writing letters of thanks.

To Diane Buchanan for being swift and skilled with her drawings.

Grateful acknowledgment is also made to the following authors and publishers and to those organizations, authors, and publishers listed in various footnotes throughout the book.

Eric Carle and Philomel for permission to use a mask based on *The Very Hungry Caterpillar*.

Paula Danziger for permission to use quotations from *The Pistachio Prescription*, Delacorte.

Frieda Gates for permission to use an adaptation of material on pages 10 and 11 of her book, *Easy to Make Costumes*.

Linda Glovach for permission to use her magic make-up recipe from *The Little Witch's Black Magic Book of Disguises*.

Formula for "looking old and wrinkled," crown shape, bullfighter's hat, and Robin Hood cap by permission of Methuen Children's Books for Gail Haley, author of *Costumes for Plays and Playing*, © 1978.

Excerpts adapted from pp. 29, 31, 32, 44, and 99 in *Quick and Easy Holiday Costumes* by Vivienne Eisner. Copyright © 1977 by Vivienne Eisner. By permission of Lothrop, Lee & Shepard Books (A Division of William Morrow & Company).

Maria Polushkin Robbins for permission to use material based on her book, *Mother, Mother, I Want Another*, Crown Publishers, Inc.

Photo on page 1 of a wild thing with the book *Where the Wild Things Are* by Maurice Sendak, Harper Junior, © Maurice Sendak. Used by permission.

Photo on page 17 of a bear with the book *The Bears' Christmas*, Random House. Used by permission Stan and Jan Berenstain.

Material on pages 21 and 28 adapted with permission of Four Winds Press, an imprint of Macmillan Publishing Company from *Easy Costumes You Don't Have to Sew* by Goldie Taub Chernoff, illustrated by Margaret Hartelius. Text, Copyright © 1977 by Goldie Taub Chernoff. Illustrations, Copyright © 1977 by Margaret Hartelius.

Photo on page 39 of Little Miss Muffet with the book *Mother Goose* by Tasha Tudor, Walck. By permission Tasha Tudor.

Photo of pigs on page 43 with the book *The Three Little Pigs* by Paul Galdone, Houghton Mifflin. By permission Paul Galdone.

Photo of skeleton on page 49 with the book *Funnybones* by Janet and Allan Ahlberg, Morrow. By permission of the original publishers, William Heinemann, Ltd.

Photo on page 50 of Big Anthony and Strega Nona with the book *Strega Nona*, copyright 1975 by Tomie dePaola. Published by Prentice-Hall. Used by permission Tomie dePaola.

Photo on page 50 of Clifford with the book *Clifford's Family* by Norman Bridwell, Scholastic. By permission Norman Bridwell.

Photo on page 51 of Curious George, the man in the big yellow hat, and hospital personnel with the book *Curious George Goes to the Hospital* by H. A. Rey, Houghton Mifflin. By permission Houghton Mifflin.

Photo on page 87 of Johnny Appleseed with the book *The Story of Johnny Appleseed* by Aliki, Prentice-Hall, Inc. By permission Aliki Brandenberg.

Photo on page 106 from *The Chandler Arizonan*, November 23, 1983. Used by permission.

I. INTRODUCTION AND SUGGESTIONS FOR USING THIS BOOK

Introduction

I LOVE CHILDREN'S BOOKS AND I like to share the joy they have brought me with others. I have spent much time, therefore, in seeking to bring books alive by reading aloud from my favorites and by engineering situations where books may be enjoyed through pantomimes, simple dramatizations, and art work.

Naturally, I have also attempted what many school librarians have promoted, namely, special events to celebrate books for which children dress up as book characters. These occasions have been enjoyed by everyone. However, such events have resulted in my being besieged by questions as to which characters could be portrayed easily and how to go about the process. I have not had a source to which to refer the teachers, parents, and students for some answers to their questions.

In addition, over some years of being involved with these celebrations with costumed characters, I had found that character creations of commercial media—TV and movies—are much more universally known than those of children's authors undiscovered by the media. I realized that the artists and artisans responsible for these film creations were experts at constructing vividly and uniquely executed images of the characters, images *bound* to be retained in the memory of any viewer, particularly when imitated in other forms for merchandising purposes. I understood all these influences on participants in the celebration of children's books. But, whether the occasion was a parade with book characters and floats, a general book character costume day for the whole school, or an introduction of a few costumed library aides at a flag raising ceremony, I was *tired* of floats representing Jaws, E.T., and the Herbie who goes to Monte Carlo; of children costumed with rubber masks depicting Henry Munster and Smurfs; and even of the inevitable representations of the Charlie Brown and Snoopy gang, popular though they all were with the onlookers.

A wild thing from *Where the Wild Things Are*.

My vision of a joyous sharing of beloved characters from the world of children's literature—a sharing which would provide an opportunity for some thinking and choices as to costume details on the part of the participants as well as provide some advertising for the related books—was being frustrated.

True, the rules I formulated, and which were generally followed, required participants to be *book* characters and to either carry the book or to have its title prominently displayed (except during guessing game celebrations in the classrooms). But Dick Tracy and Fred Flintstone were not the book characters I had in mind. True, also, there *were* notable successes in terms of my vision. One child, who wore merely a large paper sack over his head and upper body became, with the addition of gray poster paint, a few appropriate dark lines, and some yarn, a marvelous monster, unmistakably one from *Where the Wild Things Are* rather than one from a Hollywood source. True, I could even accept gladly the portrayals of characters who, having their origin in books, later achieved fame by way of the screen, such as the Mary Poppins, the Pippi Longstockings, and the characters from the *Little House* series by Wilder that kept appearing in the celebrations.

But I yearned for more successes. I tried to communicate my goals and ideas.

Of course, every year I dressed as a character from the picture book world myself. Not talented as an artist, I was particularly pleased when a student standing in the rear of the audience instantly recognized the arrangement of gray construction paper covered boxes (complete with gold tooth) that I wore over my head, and called out with glee, "Oh, it's George from *George and Martha!*" even before I brought out my chocolate chip cookies or tried to rollerskate.

Some teachers had also learned the value of role modeling. A second grade teacher wore a large spider on her straw hat and carried a stuffed toy pig under her arm, becoming a darling Fern from *Charlotte's Web*. And a first grade teacher put together her boxes for headgear, covered them with red bulletin board paper, and was transformed into a truly believable Clifford the Big Red Dog. (And, oh, it did my heart good to see the demand for "books about Clifford" that her appearance and introduction initiated.)

Nonetheless, a sparse scattering of models was not enough. I tried additional strategies. Each year, I would have pictures taken of all participants in the event. I would show all these pictures later, just for the students' enjoyment. However, an underlying motive in taking the slides was to be able to sort out a goodly number of exemplary models. The following year, I would show to classes only the cream of the crop, according to my criteria, in preparation for the coming celebration. I would point out, for example, how just one prop—the scrubbing brush—made one know without question that the character represented was Harry the Dirty Dog and not simply any old dog, not even the also black-and-white Snoopy. The use of available materials, like grocery bags, was emphasized. "See how the scraps of yarn glued around the front of the paper sack show you, without a doubt, that he's a lion?" I lectured, secretly wishing that the character had been C. S. Lewis' Aslan or the Happy Lion from the Fatio titles, rather than merely a nameless lion from the book *Wild Animals*. But I felt that I was not really communicating, a feeling that was intensified when I would ask for other ideas at the end of the presentation and would receive minimal response.

Although I probably realized that the execution of ideas would likely require adult guidance and although several times it occurred to me that my slide presentation might be given with more profitable results to the parents at the back-to-school PTO open house, I withheld from taking this approach. There was an unwillingness on my part to allow my concept of a simple celebration to snowball into a production or a competition with elaborate and/or costly costuming.

Giving up on photographed examples, I attempted another approach. I handed out cards to small groups within classes before our celebrations. On each card I had written the name of a book character I considered unique and easy enough to costume and/or imitate. The assignment for the small group was to brainstorm ideas for portraying the character and then share with the total group. The ideas were good; the concrete results were negligible. I had reached the end of my strategies, I thought.

Introduction

In faculty meeting, I appealed to the teachers to guide their students toward characters from the world of children's literature rather than those from Hollywood and TV and kept my fingers crossed. I really knew that this was not a solution to my problem, though. I knew that some teachers, those who perhaps did not read aloud to their classes, did not have the necessary exposure to the wonderful array of unforgettable and distinctive individuals that populate our current offerings for children. Other teachers who truly knew books were hindered by the false idea that exceptional creative and artistic talent was essential for the costuming.

At last, I came to the realization that I had a task—the task of providing guidance for representing book characters in a written form. I knew that excellent books on *making* costumes were already available. What was needed was a book on ways of connecting a special book character to a given costume or vice versa.

This book, then, is my final strategy. It is written with the hope that it may be used as a starting-point for teachers, librarians, and also parents to help children work out their own ideas for depicting characters from children's books.

To avoid unwieldy writing, I will refer to children as "your students"; furthermore, I will write from the point of view of the school librarian. I am sure, however, that parents and public librarians will be able to make the translations necessary to fit their own circumstances.

As you probably have surmised by now, my biases in this venture are

1. that the representation should come from original authentic children's literature as opposed to offshoots and adaptations from movies or television, and
2. that the costume should be created rather than packaged and that thought and ingenuity should be utilized rather than money.

Suggestions for Using This Book

For all librarians, teachers, and parents, I would suggest a quick reading of Chapters II and III, "Choosing and Capturing a Character" and "Putting the Costume Together." Armed with the ideas therein, you will have sufficient skill to dream up and execute your own representation of any character—more importantly, to guide children in the process. If you still have not "connected" with a character, there are dozens more in the remaining part of the book to glance over.

School Librarians. In response to questions from adult or child patrons as to how to represent a specific character, you will find easy access to the characters in the body of the book since they are listed alphabetically by character name within the broad categories of picture story books, fiction, biography, etc. The character name/character type index was mainly designed with a parent who might be unacquainted with traditional literature groupings in mind; however, it might be useful to you on those occasions when a parent has a ready-made costume in hand and is looking for a character to match it. On the other hand, your own extensive knowledge of the characters in children's literature and your own card catalog will no doubt be more inclusive.

Since you as the school librarian would often be the person coordinating book celebrations, you might consider reading the options presented in Chapter X, "What to Do with a Costumed Book Character, or, Putting on a Celebration." All, as you will see, have advantages and disadvantages. To prepare for a book parade with individual entries, you might want to select any of the listed character names to use in engineering a situation where children can brainstorm ways in which the characters could be portrayed and develop ideas on their own. Additionally, you might like to know the most recent book celebration programs at my school (for which I utilized the form for preparing a classroom entry on page 108 from the chapter, "Ideas for a Class Presentation of a Single Title") were good ones, both in terms of participation from classes and in terms of enthusiastic responses from participants and audience. (See Appendix D for the titles used in these programs.) Incidentally, adapting a form already written is usually a faster process for me, than the creation of one "from scratch." If this is the case for you, you might want to look over the appendix, specifically the entry and information forms if you are ready to launch into book celebrations.

Public Librarians. Since I feel that I am rather ignorant of the territory of the public librarian, I am hesitant to provide suggestions. I hope that this book will be useful as a reference volume for you to provide parents who are searching for ideas for characters that their children could represent, or who are seeking a character "match" for a costume they already have. I hope that you have the Chernoff/Hartelius title, *Easy Costumes You Don't Have to Sew*, in your collection as this has been the book of most use to me in the actual execution of costumes. Finally, I would surmise that any of the presentations involving costumed book characters described in Chapters X and XI would be a fitting culmination to a summer reading program or a fun interlude in the middle.

Parents. To the parent who is reading this text, I would like you to know that your effort in helping your child appreciate children's books is the prime influence in his or her road to literacy. The simple fact is enjoyment is the best motivation for reading and reading skill increases as more time is spent on reading. So, congratulations and thank you.

I would really advise parents just to ask their children to name some of their favorite book characters and to go from there. If the character name can be found in the character name/character type index, so much the better; if not, do not despair. Read Chapters II and III of this book and you will be able to help your child create his or her own representation. If your child already has a costume created or purchased for another occasion and wants to wear it, you might like to look at the character index to see if the type is listed. If not, consult your librarian and/or the card catalog.

In any case, do remember to help your child read the associated book and to decide on props or actions to make the character unique. If, as is sometimes the case, a second character should complement the first so that the identities of both will become evident to viewers, encourage your child to recruit a school friend. If you are pressed for time, look under the heading "school age children" in the character index and you will find many book characters who simply wear regular school clothing. Attention to the related book, special props, and/or partners will quickly yield a book character "costume" without time spent on construction of headgear or body coverings. Lastly, I must mention that you might like to join your child and his or her teachers in the enjoyment of a book celebration by taking part in it yourself. Recently the Ellis family at my school planned together to present *Old Black Witch*. The boy was Nicky; the girl, Old Black Witch; and the parent, Nicky's mother. Look in the character index under the heading "adults" for more suggestions. Of course, nothing says that you could not represent a child or animal character, if your own child approves.

Teachers. My last comments in this chapter are directed to the classroom teacher who reads this. I am so grateful to you, also, for your endeavors toward helping children enjoy literature. While it may be easier to spend classroom time doing multiple workbook skill sheets, it certainly is not as rewarding for the child or for yourself.

If you are pioneering book celebrations in your school, after reading Chapters II and III, read the first part of Chapter X, "What to Do with a Costumed Book Character, or Putting on a Celebration," to get started and to be fully aware of the skills you really are working on. Ask your librarian to join in the process and share in the gratification. If you would like to tie costumed book characters into social studies, Chapter VIII, "Ideas for Characters from Biography," might be of use. Preschool and kindergarten teachers, alternatively, might relish a Mother Goose Day and find some suggestions in Chapter IV, "Ideas for Characters from

Introduction

Mother Goose." If, rather than have children work either individually or in small groups on many different character representations, you would prefer to work with the whole class on a single book title at a time, you might like to read the entry form/guide for a single class entry on page 108; glance through the suggestions that follow for ways of presenting titles at your grade level; and skim the bibliography of titles for class presentations at the end of the chapter. However, be mindful that the books that your students are delighting in right now, either through their own reading or through your reading aloud to them, are the ones that should be celebrated at your school.

More power and more pleasure to you with books. I would appreciate hearing of your successes and even of your failures.

MARY WILSON
2600 South Azalea Drive
Tempe, Arizona 85282

II. CHOOSING A CHARACTER AND CAPTURING ITS ESSENCE

First and foremost, the choice of character should be one the student likes.

There is a beginning reader, *The Tale of Thomas Meade* by Pat Hutchins, to which children relate very well. I could see Thomas as an easily characterized parade entry that would greatly amuse the audience. But, since I have pretty strong negative feeling about his repetitive, impertinent "Why should I?" I could not bring myself to represent him.

I would not want to force a student into a particular character representation against his or her wishes.

If you and your students have been exploring books together, there should be no difficulty in selecting a favorite character. The problem arises when the favored character is the same one for the entire class. This is where the teacher as psychologist comes in. "There are so many different, wonderful characters in our books, that it would be a shame to concentrate only on one everybody already knows. Perhaps you might like to think about your 'second best' character." Or, in the case of a choice of Snoopy or E.T.: "Let's help Mrs. Wilson advertise some books that all the kids don't already know about." Still several students wanting the same character? In such situations I frequently resort to the "choose a number" technique. (The student with the number closest to the teacher's would get to represent the character.) The remaining students may be guided into consideration of other characters from the same title to go along with the character for which they had genuine affection but from which they were thwarted.

Do not worry about the mechanics of costuming at this point in helping your students make choices, unless time restraints dictate attention to this facet of the process. The focus of the next chapter will be on putting the costume together and it will deal with mechanics.

In confession, for years I have been delighted by the antics of Hoban's character Frances, and the students have joined me in my affection for this quintessential, lovable "child." But, until fairly recently, I have absolutely groaned at the idea of costuming a *badger*! Now I know how—and you will, too. So do help children with their choice of character without too much regard for anticipated difficulty with the execution of the costuming. Ideas on the communication to the audience of what the character is all about *are* what is essential at this stage of planning a book character presentation.

Ask your students what book character they remember most vividly from their own reading or from being read aloud to. Ask them, "Is there something special about that character that no one else in the whole world wears, has, does, or says? Something that is as distinctive and unique as a person's signature?" These questions are the key to learning how to represent a character so that others will recognize and enjoy the representation.

I call the answers to these questions the "essence" of the character. Essence is that which makes a thing what it is. For example, although there are many ghosts in children's literature, if I capture the essence of one particular ghost, you will know his name, if you have read the book.

I will dress this particular ghost in the traditional white sheet; put a sheriff's badge on him (a piece of yellow construction paper cut in the shape of a star will do); and have him carry a stuffed black cat and/or a homemade cardboard owl. Do you recognize him now? Of

Choosing a Character

course, it's Georgie, along with Herman and Miss Oliver, from the charming series by Robert Bright.

Only sheets with various prints available to you? Well, then you have a perfect costume for Gus, from the book, *Gus Was a Gorgeous Ghost*, by Jane Thayer. I hope you and your student will remember to have Gus carry along a box of watercolors and a brush to help express *his* essence.

Of course, it *is* permissible to exaggerate a character's attributes to make sure effective communication with an audience takes place. For example, bunny rabbits are extremely common in children's literature. But an ordinary rabbit costume is quickly turned into an instantly identifiable version of one of the most winning of picture story book characters by the addition of a single exaggerated prop. The character? Little Rabbit from the book *Little Rabbit's Loose Tooth*. The prop? A tooth, made from tagboard and practically filling the child's mouth, that is capable of being wiggled. (Bugs Bunny's big teeth do *not* wiggle.)

All of the examples above have been taken from the picture book genre, however, and picture story book characters are usually more distinctive than characters that appear in longer fiction. Frequently, capturing the essence of these characters from fiction for identification by an audience is more difficult, but the problem is not insurmountable.

Once again, an example will be detailed: Even more numerous than ghosts and rabbits in children's literature are the dozens of conventional, everyday, school age children who appear in fiction titles. No one would be at all interested in someone parading at a book celebration in everyday school clothes unless something else is added. This is where one has to think of especially funny or unhappy situations these characters have lived through, the predicaments they have survived.

Suppose a boy, dressed in regular school clothes, was carrying a cardboard box, labelled "Try Our Large Economy Size." And suppose a large stuffed dog, too big for the box to accommodate comfortably, was in it. The boy would also be holding a dime in his teeth (a large fake one, please, with a printed 10¢ in full view). If you have read this Beverly Cleary title, you most likely will be able to place our boy as Henry Huggins, trying to get Ribsy home with him on the bus.

The portrayal of Henry could be made more dramatic. Perhaps you might consider using a live dog, stuffed in a shopping bag, with paper loosely tied over his protruding head. As related in the book, Henry would find the dog so heavy that he would carry the shopping bag with one handle in each hand. Or, Henry's friend Scooter, heckling him about the contents of the bag, might be added to the presentation. A fall by Henry could be staged as his dog escapes from the sack. A more ambitious undertaking would be to include the bus driver and several of the passengers. Henry's fall in trying to catch the freed Ribsy would jostle the other passengers into dropping the items they are carrying. These may include any or all of the bag of apples, the pots and pans, the books (please be gentle!), and the hose described by Cleary. The bus driver expressing anger and a siren sound indicating the approach of the police car would top off the action.

Obviously, pairs of children and small groups work well in depicting some books. Recently at my school, Bates' Little Rabbit was joined by her tooth fairy, complete with ears, wings, and wand.

Perhaps the following list will help you and your students practice focusing on some of the possibilities that are available in representing the essence of a book character so that character is revealed to a viewer.

Pinocchio
Little Bo Peep
the third little pig

> Frances (the badger from the Hoban books)
> Lentil (from McCloskey's book of the same name)
> Ellen Tebbits (title and person from Beverly Cleary's series)
> Cassie Stephens from *The Pistachio Prescription* by Paula Danziger

Now, look at this list and see if you would have chosen any of these "props" to represent the character's specialty:

> a long false nose
> a shepherd's crook and toy stuffed lamb
> a brick and a trowel or a cauldron or model thereof, labelled "wolf pot"
> a slice of bread and jam, either real or giant-sized tagboard variety; or a plastic tea set; or a plate of soft eggs
> a harmonica
> a lumpy roll of underwear or a pair of chalkboard erasers laden with dust
> sunglasses and pistachio nuts (or a bag labelled so)

You may have different memories of these characters, leading you to different and even better choices for props. In any case, you have probably discovered that once the character is read about and examined—really known—it is fun and relatively easy to think of the something special that would suggest the character to an onlooker.

Incidentally, one big help in deciding on what will communicate the essence of a character is the illustration chosen for the dust jacket or the front cover of the book. Frequently, but not always, the publishers have done the work for you. For example, Peter, from *Tales of a Fourth Grade Nothing*, is shown balancing Dribble in his bowl, up high, out of Fudgie's determined reach, summing up the plot and characterizations beautifully.

In general, for an audience to be able to identify the character, it is best to choose a *named* character; that is, someone (anthropomorphized animal or otherwise) endowed with enough personality to have been given a name by the author. There are quite a few exceptions to this guideline, however. I can think of the boy from Tresselt's *The Mitten*, identified only as "my grandfather" in the story, who would be instantly recognizable in a book celebration, carrying a huge red mitten filled to overflowing with stuffed animals. "Little Girl" from Harper's *The Gunniwolf* and the funny little woman from Mosel's Caldecott Award book, neither of whom has a regular name, have distinctive "essences" and similarly could be easily characterized for viewing. On the other hand, the grandfathers, little girls, and women in *A Sweetheart for Valentine*, for example, seem too nondescript to consider portraying.

Some books, though, are peopled by nameless but visually very distinctive characters which I could heartily endorse for book celebrations. I am thinking of a book like *Cloudy with a Chance of Meatballs*. A representation of the people with their plates and umbrellas extended to catch what is falling from the latest weather would make a readily identifiable presentation and certainly a positive celebration of children's literature.

Indeed, even *inanimate* objects, with no personality whatsoever, may be represented profitably by children for a festival honoring books. It is usually best if they are paired with the appropriate *real* character, however. To elucidate, the cat from "Hey, Diddle, Diddle" may be accompanied by a child wearing the fiddle. The character of Harold from *Harold and the Purple Crayon* practically insists on being supplemented by a student dressed as a purple crayon. Representing the giant jam sandwich from Lord's book of the same name would make for an entertaining parade entry, but a wasp should be added also, and so on.

The point is that the character chosen should have either a distinct personality or a unique appearance. Such criteria would rule out many of the very beginning readers as

Choosing a Character

sources for characters as well as other books with bland, less than top quality characterization and illustration.

Although I find that I like to work from my chosen character to the costume, I know that sometimes children have costumes already at hand and, of course, want to wear them. In this case, consulting the card catalog or your librarian would most likely yield some suitable stories with characters "to match" the costume. Once the stories are located, they should be read, of course, and the one with the most appeal to the student should be selected. Again, as soon as a particular named character who would normally wear the costume can be identified and chosen, the principle of determining the essence of the character in terms of items, attributes, or actions would be followed.

Some named characters that just might fit costumes already available to students will be found listed on pages 34–35 of the next chapter. Suggestions for characters to match the three costumes that have appeared most frequently at the celebrations at my school will follow and conclude this chapter.

It is easy to understand why there is a prevalence of ghost, witch, and rabbit costumes at book character festivities. Children commonly have ghost and witch costumes left in their possession from Halloween outings. And a rabbit outfit is one of the easiest to make; ears and tail are all that are really necessary. Taking just these three costumes as a starting point, I will examine what can be done to portray individual characters clearly, as well as point out some ramifications that might proceed from the titles.

Parenthetically, some of the characters in the listing that follow could not be retrieved by using the card catalog since awareness of their existence depends on more detailed knowledge of the contents of a children's collection than is accessed by the catalog. In other words, if you have no success in finding a character to match a certain costume by using the card catalog, do consult your librarian.

Ghosts

Fudge from *Superfudge* (Blume).

Fudgie is really a very undistinguishable ghost going trick or treating. But add Peter in beard and moustache, mask with black-rimmed glasses and large rubber nose, and "Grandfather Hatcher's hat" and Alex Santo in a sheet or sandwich board replication of the painting *Anita's Anger*, and the nondescript ghost becomes a known person. Naturally, trick or treat bags would be carried by all three characters.

Georgie (Bright).

Each title calls for different treatment of costuming details. From *Georgie's Halloween*, Georgie would wear a first prize ribbon, presented to him by a mouse. A child for Herman, in a cat costume with face mask and neck bow, and one for Miss Oliver, dressed as an owl wearing a witch's hat, could accompany Georgie. Georgie could pretend to blow out the candle in a jack-o'-lantern as in the story.

For *Georgie and the Robbers* one would include the two masked crooks, carrying a hammer and a crank, and perhaps, also, the cow.

Georgie Goes West would require the addition of Kio, the Hopi Indian boy, and perhaps the pinto pony, Little Lightning. Of course, Georgie would be wearing a feather bonnet for this title.

Finally, a portrayal of *Georgie and the Noisy Ghost* would have Georgie banging twelve times on a frying pan with a spoon. For a more in-depth presentation, Captain Hooper would be costumed with his pirate hat, boots, and sword, or, more easily accomplished, in pirate hat, nightshirt, and slippers; and he would howl seven times. A costumed grandfather clock could strike the hour of twelve before Captain Hooper's appearance. Or, the complete incident of waking the sleeping Captain could be enacted, with Herman trying to arouse him by mewing, Miss Oliver by hooting, and Georgie finally being successful with his striking of the spoon on the frying pan. The howling and the presentation of medals to the Captain would follow.

If your student's choice is just to represent Georgie by himself, having him carry a board and a hinge and make the sound effects to represent his creaking the stairs and squeaking the parlor door would show his identity.

Cloud Men from *James and the Giant Peach* (Dahl).

The cloud men have "two piercing black eyes." They could be painting rainbows; making thunder with hammers on drums; and/or carrying a machine labelled "snow machine." The addition of some or all of the friends from the giant peach, watching them and pretending fear, would be fun.

Rabbit from *Homer the Hunter* (Margolis).

In representation of this character a child in rabbit costume would have a sheet draped over the costume and be dancing around a Homer, saying, "I'm a Ghost Rabbit come back to haunt you. OOOOOOOOOO." Homer would be wearing his hunting clothes and be carrying a shotgun.

Mr. Penny from *The Ghost with the Halloween Hiccups* (Mooser).

Mr. Penny would be wearing his ghost robe over his body and have his head piece draped over his arm. He would sport a moustache, wear a tiny fedora, have just a fringe of hair on his bald (nylon stocking) head, and be emitting loud hiccups. "Happy HIC CUP Halloween!" Any or all of following characters who try to help him cure his hiccups could be added: Laura and Bert with their water; Mrs. Gates with her suggestion of singing with a paper bag on his head; Mr. Brown with his feather to tickle Mr. Penny's nose (HIC CUP! AH-CHOO! HIC CUP!); Mayor Bell with her hopping idea, etc. Or, just the scare from Laura and Bert costumed as a bat and a dragon could be portrayed.

Rob from *Soup and Me* (Peck).

Rob is just a plain Halloween ghost who could not be identified by himself. He needs his buddy, Soup, along. In the chapter, "Havoc on Halloween," Soup was dressed as a pirate with eye patch, moustache, wood sword, and cardboard from ankle to knee. Both could be pushing the "biggest pumpkin in the State of Vermont" in a wheelbarrel, followed by farmer Sutter with his switch in his hand.

Gus from *Gus Was a Friendly Ghost* (Thayer).

For this title one would have Gus providing a toasted cheese sandwich or a box of macaroni and cheese for his friend, Mouse.

Treatment of *Gus Was a Gorgeous Ghost* might be more detailed. To be accurate, his sheet would be covered with multi-colored bats, owls, footprints, etc. He could carry a potato ready for printing or be consulting a large replica of "The Laws of Ghostdom." Perhaps he could be joined by Madame Richardson in a lesson on potato printing.

Boris from *Halloween with Morris and Boris* (Wiseman).

Bear headgear (see next chapter) for Boris would be partially covered by the ghost sheet. Boris would say "Boo" to Morris who would respond with a "Yeeeowoo! You ARE a ghost!" and run. Or Morris could just accompany Boris in *his* Halloween costume, the one created by his encounter with the trash can, complete with an inner tube around his neck, a tomato can hanging on his antler, and a striped tie on his rear.

Witches

Humbug Witch from *Humbug Witch* (Balian).

For this character only the witch's hat would be used. A commercial mask with a large nose could be utilized. Long red hair would be nice to add. Other items of Humbug Witch's clothing include a black shawl, plaid apron, red polka dot bloomers, orange gloves, and red-and white-striped stockings. (Of course, an approximation of the clothing would be fine.) She could carry a large pot and some pickle juice or peanut butter perhaps. She could also be accompanied by a child in cat headgear or a stuffed black cat with his name tag, "Fred," hanging around his neck.

Ramona from *Ramona the Pest* (Cleary).

For the kindergarten Halloween party Ramona would be wearing a commercial rubber witch's mask and a regular black witch's robe. She would be identified by the kindergarten-style printed sign that Ramona pinned on herself, which included Ramona's distinctive Q turned into a cat. A Susan could be added for Ramona to "boing" her curls.

Dorrie from various titles by Coombs.

Dorrie wears a short black dress and her trademarks are mismatched socks (one striped, one plain) and hat worn crookedly. She could be accompanied by her black cat, named Gink, and her mother, The Big Witch, who would be looking into her crystal ball.

To represent *Dorrie and the Blue Witch*, for example, Dorrie could carry a bottle labeled "shrinking powder" and she could be presented with a gold cauldron, the sign on which would read

To Dorrie

First Prize for Witch-Catching

in honor of her capture of Mildred, the Blue Witch.

For *Dorrie and the Witch's Imp*, a fight could be staged between Dorrie and Natter, her conjured look alike (but one whose stockings match). The old witch Gloris, dressed in grey and wearing a white apron, could be an onlooker, holding her Wither-Wort, labelled, of course.

Old Black Witch from Devlin's titles.

This witch is dressed as a traditional one. She would appear, from the title *Old Black Witch*, in an apron, stirring up a bowl of blueberry pancakes, happily singing her chant about pancake making.

As an alternate idea, she could be carrying two toads in a cage. Or, her first appearance to Nicky could be dramatized. She would arrive, covered with soot, stamping around and shaking her broom in a vile temper tantrum, complaining bitterly to Nicky, who would have his matches and kindling, about his building a fire.

Even more drama could be extracted from *Old Black Witch Rescues Halloween*. Mr. Butterbean, who wanted to banish Halloween, could pour a pitcher of water on Old Black Witch, yelling, "Troublemaker!" Or, Old Black Witch herself, in her typical mood of temper, could chant the formula for turning Mr. Butterbean into a green frog. A quick substitution for Mr. Butterbean would loudly croak, "Groink!"

Blue-Nosed Witch from *The Blue-Nosed Witch* (Embry).

Of course, this witch has a bright blue nose as well as the traditional broom and black cat. She could appear alone using a soft brush to polish her nose while looking in a mirror. Or, she could be accompanied by three of the witches from her group: Grande Madame, riding a vacuum cleaner; Minnie Max, sporting long blood red fingernails; and Josephine, showing her long yellow fluorescent teeth. The black pennant on which Scurry No. 13 would be printed would be good to make to identify the group. The Blue-Nosed Witch could also be included with a group of children dressed for Halloween—a ghost; a pirate; a cowboy with a six-shooter and lighted pumpkin; and a gypsy with spangled earrings—and be chased by Mr. Skinner brandishing a slingshot.

Felina from *The Little Leftover Witch* (Laughlin).

Felina could merely be walking, dressed in a regular witch costume, carrying a sign

> **My birthday is Oct. 31**
> **(gift from George P. Doon, Sr.)**

or she could be stamping her foot and saying, "Witches never comb their hair!" The latter action would be most effective if Felina were accompanied by a loving mother (Mrs. Doon) waving a hairbrush and Mrs. Doon's little girl, Lucinda, trying to reach her with a comb. Felina would exit with an arms-on-hips pose, saying disgustedly, "Bats and cats!"

Witch from *Hansel and Gretel*.

The traditionally dressed hag could be beckoning with her finger and offering a luscious piece of candy. A child costumed as her gingerbread house would clinch the representation. Hansel and Gretel could be added to the picture, of course. See page 44 for other details.

Rabbits

Rabbit from *Who's in Rabbit's House?* (Aardema).

Rabbit, if true to the book, would wear rabbit headgear but the rest of his body would be covered by an over-one-shoulder short dress. Another child could wear rabbit's house and would use a "bad voice" to threaten rabbit and his friends. The story is perfect for a dramatization that would include the frog, jackal, leopard, elephant, rhinoceros, and the long green caterpillar.

Orson Abbott from *The Easter Egg Artists* (Adams).

Orson could have his arms full of the oversized "comic" eggs that he invented. He could be painting beautiful designs on a model airplane or a car or he could simply carry a giant replica of a set of paints and a paintbrush.

Grandfather Stupid from *The Stupids Have a Ball* (Allard).

Grandfather Stupid, his white beard and moustache showing, attends the ball dressed as the Easter Bunny. As mixed up as the other members of his family, he also carries a large pumpkin and booms out, "Ho, ho, ho!"

Little Rabbit from *The Little Rabbit Who Wanted Red Wings* (Bailey).

Little Rabbit, with pink ears and red eyes, would also sport red wings. He could be accompanied by the inspiration for the red wings—the redbird—and by all those who do not

Choosing a Character

recognize him in his changed state: Mr. Bushy Tail, the grey squirrel; Mrs. Porcupine, in glasses; Miss Puddle Duck, wearing her red rubbers; and his mother. Little Rabbit could be crying until Mr. Groundhog offers his solution to the problem.

Little Rabbit from *Little Rabbit's Loose Tooth* (Bate).
   Little Rabbit would have an oversized tagboard tooth, attached so it could be wiggled. The tooth could also appear, however, on top of a spoonful of chocolate ice cream dished up from Little Rabbit's bowl. An alternate idea might be to have Little Rabbit, the hole (blackened tooth) showing in her mouth, withdrawing a foil-covered tagboard circle, labelled 10¢, from a large envelope. The rabbit tooth fairy, her wings in place and wand in hand, could be hovering around Little Rabbit during this process.

Wilbur from *The Bionic Bunny Show* (Lauren Krasny Brown and Marc Brown).
   Wilbur would wear a T-shirt, shorts, tights, and a red cape. Football shoulder pads and stuffing for enlarged biceps and a large orange "B" on his T-shirt would turn him into the Bionic Bunny. He also needs an oversized "bionic" wristwatch with a TV-like screen on it and headgear that would support two large upright bunny ears separated by a red antenna on a red base. He could twitch his nose if a box headgear is not used and perhaps a contrivance made of thread could be used to make the ears wiggle. He could be leaping and showing off his muscles to an attendant cameraperson or he could carry a large mockup of the pussy cat, making two masked rat robbers scramble.

Little bunny from *Runaway Bunny* (Margaret Wise Brown).
   Each incident in this story would present alternate costuming possibilities. A fun choice would be to have the little bunny pretending to swim. Mother rabbit, carrying a fisherman's bag and net, would be holding a fishing pole and dangling the carrot on the end of its line in front of little bunny's nose.

White Rabbit from *Alice's Adventures in Wonderland* (Carroll).
   The White Rabbit would be wearing a waistcoat from which he would extract a large pocket watch. He would say, "Oh dear, oh dear. I shall be too late" and run off quickly.

Hare from *The Hare and the Tortoise*.
   This rabbit might be pretending to run vigorously, panting with the strain. He really would be running in place, however. He would be edged out to a finish line by a tortoise, to the accompaniment of cheers from some onlookers.

Peter from *The Adventures of Peter Rabbit* (Potter).
   Peter could appear alone, wearing his blue jacket and carrying bunches of either real or oversized tagboard models of carrots and radishes in one hand. He could be rubbing his tummy with the other hand and be groaning at the same time. Alternatively, he could be chased by Mr. McGregor, who would be shaking his hoe at him menacingly. Or, he could be escorted by his mother, who would wear an apron and hold a bottle labelled "camomile tea." She would be offering a tablespoon dose of it to Peter, who would be making a face, shaking his head, and trying to say, "No."

Mr. Rabbit from *Mr. Rabbit and the Lovely Present* (Zolotow).
   Mr. Rabbit has no distinguishing characteristics. He requires a partner in order to be known. An appropriate partner is very simple to supply, however. The little girl, in flat hat, jacket and skirt, would carry a basket containing an apple, a banana, a Bartlett pear (green), and some blue grapes. She could be thanking him and waving goodbye.

There are many other ghosts, witches, and rabbits to be found in stories for children. But there are hundreds of other different characters that can be retrieved from your memory, or, if necessary, from the drawers of the card catalog.

I suspect that you are more than ready now to guide students in listing some of their own remembered book characters and in brainstorming on those specialties and props that capture and convey the essences of the characters to the audience. Enjoy the process.

III. PUTTING THE COSTUME TOGETHER

AS I HAVE MENTIONED PREVIOUSLY, for me, it is more logical and more satisfying to start with the idea of the character and then work on the costume and search for props. Within the classroom population, it is gratifying to find that even though the individual who is planning to be Johnny Appleseed knows that his or her mother will not part with a pot for the occasion, another child is as certain his or hers will. The planning and the search become a happy classroom time, utilizing creative thinking skills and fostering the good feelings that cooperation and sharing for common goals yield. Of course, if the classroom resources do not suffice, an advertisement during morning announcements usually produces results.

Always having had a "dress-up" box for our own children during their growing years, I found it invaluable to dip into for assorted items for book character costumes. Naturally, I appropriated it permanently when our girls grew to adulthood. I also added the large swatches of fabric left over from my sewing days to the huge straw hamper containing the other treasures. This became a wonderful source for red capes for Little Red Riding Hood, lacy trains to hang from the crown of the princess who slept on a pea, shoes for Cinderella, and brown slacks and top to cover the body of Curious George. The height of success as far as audiences were concerned, however, was derived from two of our daughters' outgrown dresses, still hanging in the closet, too beloved to discard to charity. One was a deep rose-colored, flowery, cotton print, complete with dainty white collar and cuffs and nipped in waist. The other was a red and white knit sack, with horizontal stripes. What was so interesting about two such rather ordinary dresses? Well, they were worn by two library aides who had made the supreme sacrifice for the promotion of books—two rugged *male* library aides, who later complained how cold it was wearing dresses in the chill November air. They represented Soup and Rob, from Robert Newton Peck's book *Soup and Me*, dressed in the clothes they had retrieved from the Baptist church Ladies Aid rummage barrel after Janice Riker had stolen their regular clothing while they were skinny dipping. As might have been expected, Janice was present also, running from them, her arms full of boys' clothing. Also delighting the audience and completing the presentation were insults, hurled in both directions.

Although I highly recommend similar accumulations of clothing and accessories for the classroom, one does not have to be a pack rat librarian to be able to put together completely satisfactory costumes. Much can be done just during the weekly art period with the almost always available school supplies, such as colored construction paper, bulletin board paper, tagboard, glue, scissors, and paint. No scrap yarn with which to make a lion's mane? Strokes of orange poster paint on a grocery bag will suffice. Signs are almost as good as the real thing, and the sign-making provides an excellent opportunity to motivate neat printing and correct spelling. Perhaps your school individual classroom budgets do not allow for such purchases as aluminum foil to cover the Tin Man. Tubes of tagboard and the characteristic funnel-shaped hat made out of tagboard will convey the message as to the character's identity, or a parent might be willing to cover the minimal cost of the foil.

How different people treated the costuming of Charlotte, from *Charlotte's Web*, is an example of working successfully with what one has. In my dress-up box I had a discarded black jersey turtleneck top and a pair of very old black pants. The library aide who wore them also took three long, narrow, white cardboard dowel-shaped sticks I had, source unknown, wrapped them in black, and tied them together in a spread position, threading yarn between them to make her web. A classroom teacher, for another event, simply had her third grade student cut a large circle from bulletin board paper. (No, it was not evenly cut but it did not matter.) The circle was large enough to cover his whole body. To it, he had attached eight small rectangles sticking out from the edges for legs. A string suspended it around his neck. He made a marvelous spider. And I like to think that the teacher utilized the teachable moment to have him look up the characteristics, or, at least, the number of legs that spiders have. (Yes, Charlotte's real legs were gray and had seven sections, but this costume communicates.)

Many body costumes can be made simply by cutting and draping bulletin board paper. Another teacher used the same principle as utilized in the second Charlotte to help one of her students be a lovely peach for *James and the Giant Peach;* other students have used paper for kingly robes and sashes. Likewise, many head coverings can be made from paper sacks and cardboard boxes available at no cost. In other words, even if your sources for materials are minimal, with some thought and time, satisfactory costumes can be created.

Top: A Berenstain bear; *bottom:* Arthur, from *Arthur's Halloween*.

I tell the students that with the appropriate head, one does not really have to worry whether or not the clothing below matches Charles' crocodile green head, for instance, or whether one's hands are covered with yellow mittens, paper or otherwise, to make them into the paws of a lion. The details are nice to complete but are not essential as the viewers' eyes go mainly to the head.

Headgear, then, is the highest priority for many costumes. There are several options for head coverings. The simplest is a circle, a piece of tagboard or a paper plate. It may be attached to a popsicle stick, a dowel, or a wooden spoon so the student may hold it in front of his or her face. These are basically what are usually called stick puppets. They may be decorated with rabbit or mouse ears and whiskers as the character requires. Noses may be drawn on the circle or made three-dimensional and taped on. One year, a talented fifth grade student shaped and drew the face for Marc Brown's Arthur the aardvark, out of heavy cardboard. It was extremely effective.

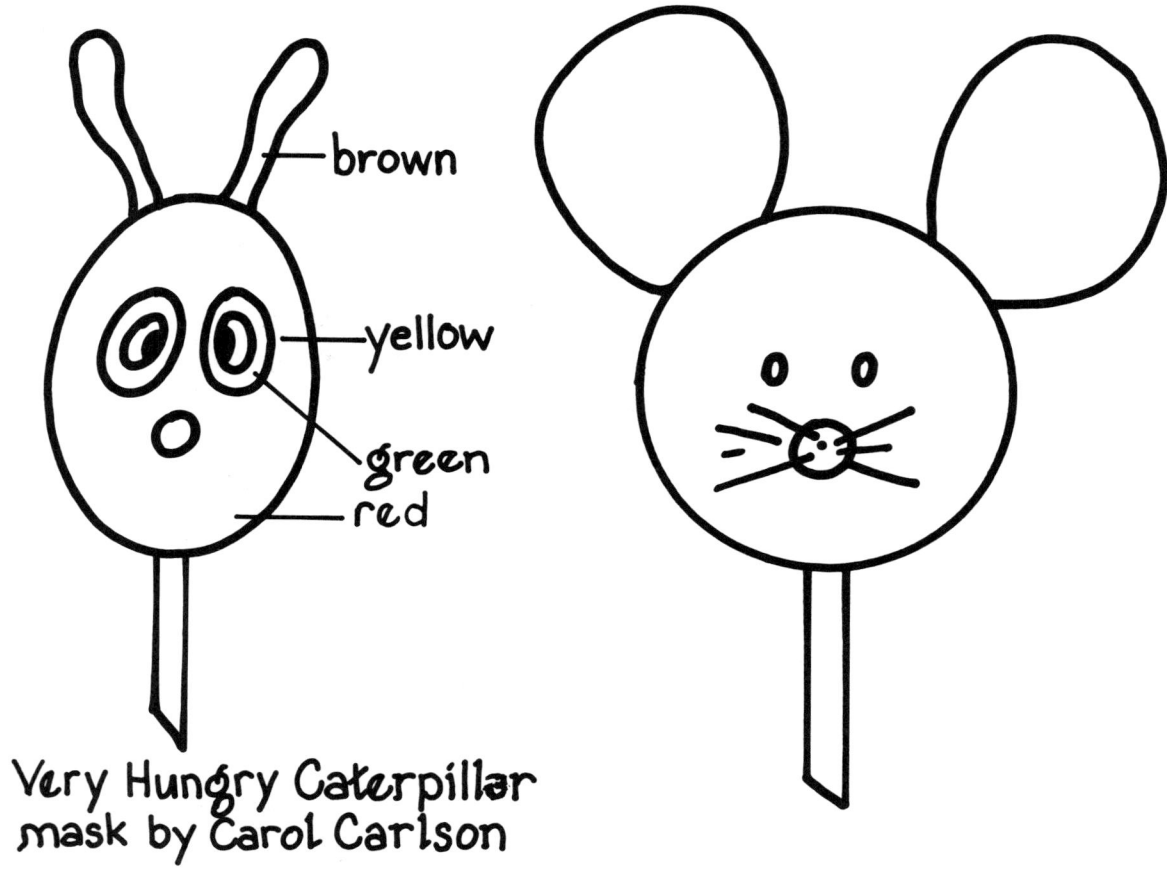

(Mask makers interested in artistic perfection would gain much from *Paper Masks and Puppets for Stories, Songs and Plays* by Ron and Marsha Feller, published by The Arts Factory, P.O. Box 55547, Seattle, WA 98155.)

Putting the Costume Together 19

Cone shaped nose as for mouse

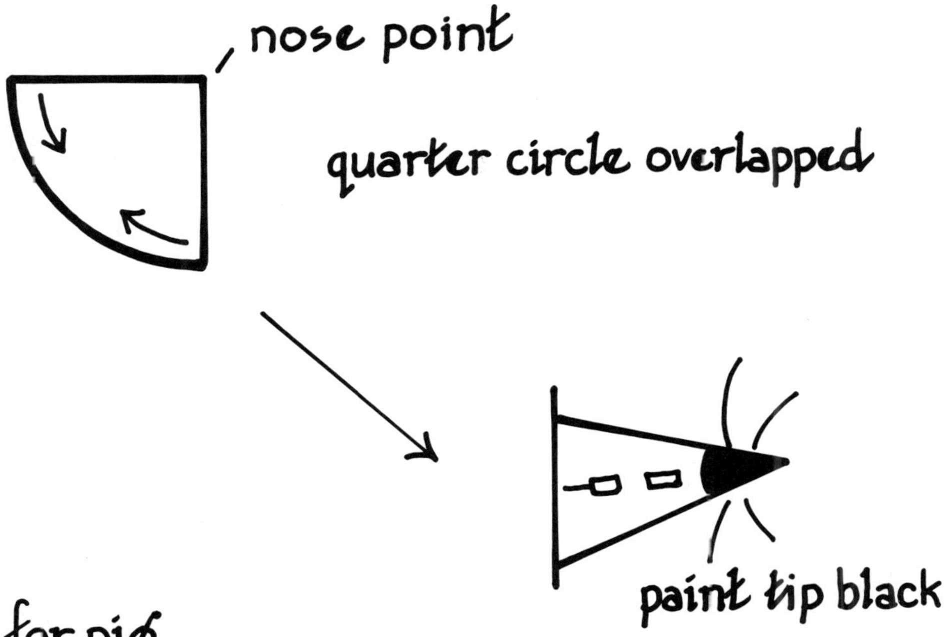

nose point

quarter circle overlapped

paint tip black

Snout, as for pig

A paper cup will work too.

The construction paper or tagboard nose may be slit in several places at the edge that attaches to the mask and the resulting tabs glued to secure the nose in place.

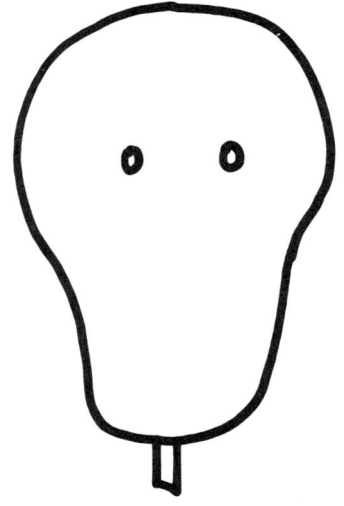

skull shape for
skeletons in **Funnybones**

A paper plate base, for firmness, can be extended with a shape cut from construction paper and pasted on top. The larger size mask that ensues is usually more impressive as well as a better color.

If such face masks are tied around the head, eyeholes are necessary. Since the measurement for the placing of the holes is a bit tricky and since safety and usually expression is lessened with eyeholes, perhaps the hand-held style is best for young elementary students. On the other hand, teacher/pedlar Betty Wilson was able to create a brown construction paper mask that was both safe and expressive for her 25 kindergartners to wear in playing the monkeys from *Caps for Sale*. In the diagram on page 57, note the wide space to view through and the earpieces. The use of pipe cleaners (in actuality bumpy chenille was the craft material utilized) rather than string allowed the children to fit their masks in place all by themselves, no minor consideration in costuming large numbers of children.

Probably the next simplest head covering after the face mask is the grocery sack. The sack may be drawn on, pasted on, or muzzles and snouts may be added with smaller sacks.

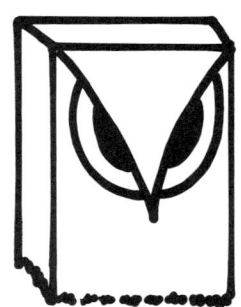
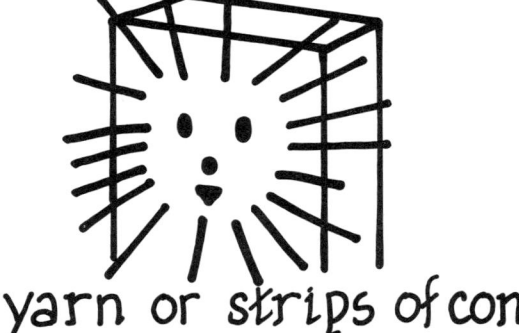

yarn or strips of construction paper for mane

Putting the Costume Together 21

Additionally, Nancy Renfro, for example, shows fake fur eyebrows and includes large ears for her bloodthirsty beast made from a grocery sack in *Bags Are Big!* The technique for muzzle and snout making is shown with admirable clarity in Chernoff's *Easy Costumes You Don't Have to Sew*.

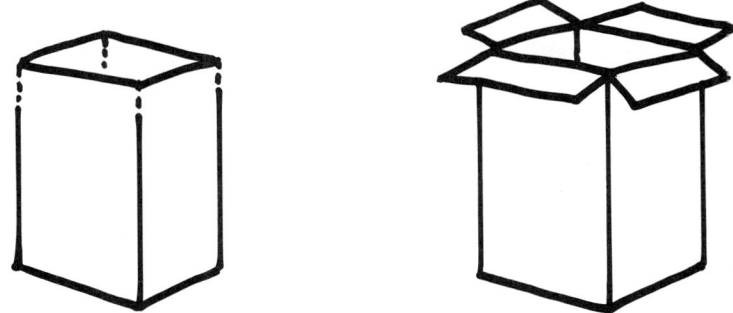

"Cut a slit in each corner of the bag and fold back to make tabs as shown. Glue or tape the tabs in place."

The nice part about an additional bag is that the eyeholes may be inconspicuous slits just above the nose, while the actual eyes of the character are in a different location, undamaged by breaks in the continuity of the paper.

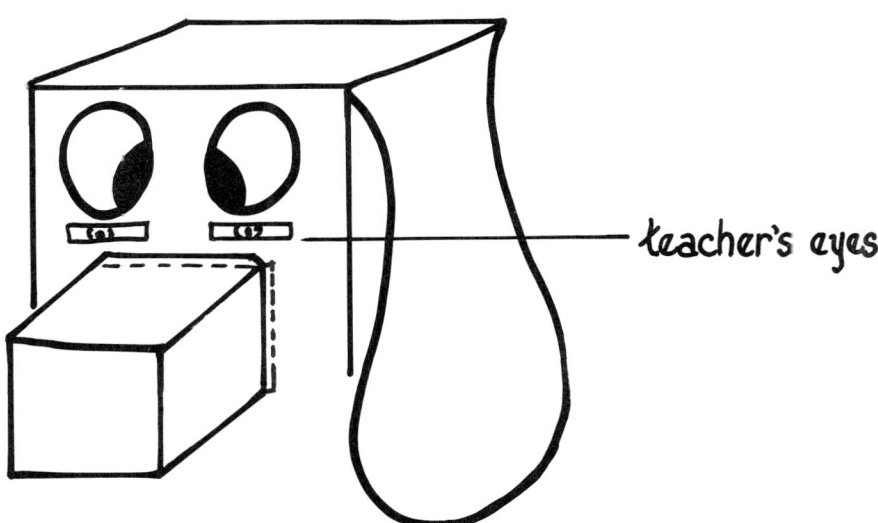

Nancy Grubb's Clifford the Big Red Dog

Even without the nose in place, however, it is more effective to keep eye slits separate from where the character's eyes are placed.

Another tip for eyeholes (one that could have avoided a couple of falls at my school by children in the ever-present ghost costumes had I known about it earlier) is given by Frieda Gates in her *Easy to Make Costumes*. She shows a method of allowing for visibility through the mouth. A cereal box—in the case of the ghost, with the two top corners cut off—is placed on top of the child's head and tied on. The sheet is glued to the cereal box to prevent slipping. Sheer fabric (dark in the case of the ghost) is taped over the mouth hole, which becomes the spot from which the child is able to see.

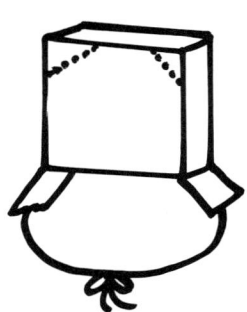 

Even if this method is not utilized, the placement of the slits for the eyes should be determined first, and they should be cut before face details are tackled. Where to cut is a bit of a problem. For the very young child, the sack will go over the shoulders and body. Have your student settle the sack comfortably and then feel for his or her eye sockets, marking the spot to be cut after the sack is removed. For comfortable fitting of the paper sack at the shoulders for the larger child, a curved section may be removed from each side. The bag may have to be shortened, as well, to fit satisfactorily. Following this fitting, the position of the eyes would be located.

For young students, paper sacks, their appearance altered by the use of paint, markers, or crayons, seem to be the most manageable choice of headgear. For students approaching young adult size, however, one may have to go to cardboard boxes to adequately represent the size of the head in proportion to the student's body. (Do remember the half circle cuts from the sides so the box can fit over the shoulders and be securely positioned.)

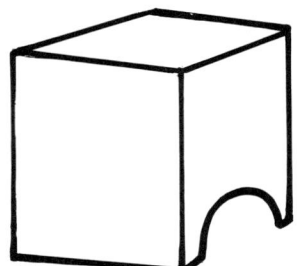 fits over the shoulders

In addition to their superiority for proportion requirements, boxes, with their heavier weight, yield a second advantage over paper sacks. The sturdier sides allow for easy wrapping of colored bulletin board paper or gluing of construction paper over them, usually making a neater effect than efforts with paint on sacks. Incidentally, I *have* cut colored construction paper to fit grocery bags and then rubber cemented it in place for my own costumes, but I feel that the manual skills required for this technique may be beyond primary graders.

Putting the Costume Together

Not everyone could duplicate the box headgear made by our school's library clerk, René Wiley. She covered the box with thin foam rubber, attaching a trunk and large ears also made of foam, and spray painted everything gray. With models of some cheese and a pickle in her hands, which were also covered by tubes of grey foam, she represented El from *Pumpernickle Tickle and Mean Green Cheese*.

But certainly, all ages have the skill necessary to glue a cut out face of a cat, a mouse, or whatever onto a cardboard box base.

Similarly, another type of head covering that is easily managed by children and that is readily available (if you are a saver, that is) is discarded nylon stockings. One use for these is in making a child instantly bald. A good monkey head for Curious George was made simply by tying a cap of nylon materials under the child's chin. Brown construction paper ears were easily pinned in place, the tension under the chin keeping them in place.

Using the nylon stocking over the face like a ski mask, with holes for eyes and ears cut out, makes the head of a Dr. Seuss character, such as a Sneetch, if you add the necessary feathery tufts on top of the head from some other materials. The nylons, if gathered at the nape of the neck, become a uniform hairpiece for each of the five Chinese brothers. For more elaborate projects, such as a red yarn wig for a Raggedy Ann or Andy or the red-fringed hair of a clown, the nylon stocking provides a secure base for construction. Such efforts are time-consuming but are basically rather simple to do.

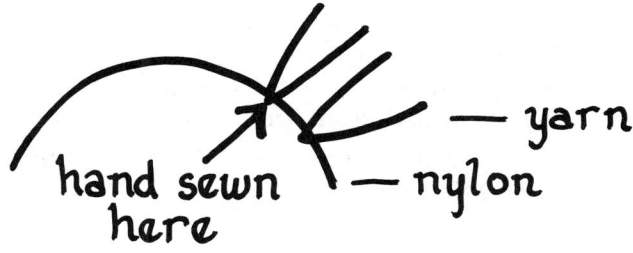

Of course, if your scavenger hunt or treasure box search yields a hooded sweatshirt, you will find that this is just the thing on which various kinds of details, such as hair, ears, or top knots, can be anchored.

Exploration of headgear possibilities would not be complete without some mention of hats. Here construction paper frequently comes to the rescue.

The trademark hat of the Cat in the Hat is easily made. One piece of construction paper (red) is lapped over to fit the child's head size and this is anchored with tape. (A bit more accuracy is obtained by taking a measurement with a tape measure around the head, just above the eyebrows. Then 1" is added to this figure to allow for ½" overlap of both ends.) The resulting cylinder of construction paper is then placed on another piece of construction paper just to outline the exact circumference of the cylinder. It is then removed and an outer circle is drawn around this first circle, to establish the perimeter of the brim.

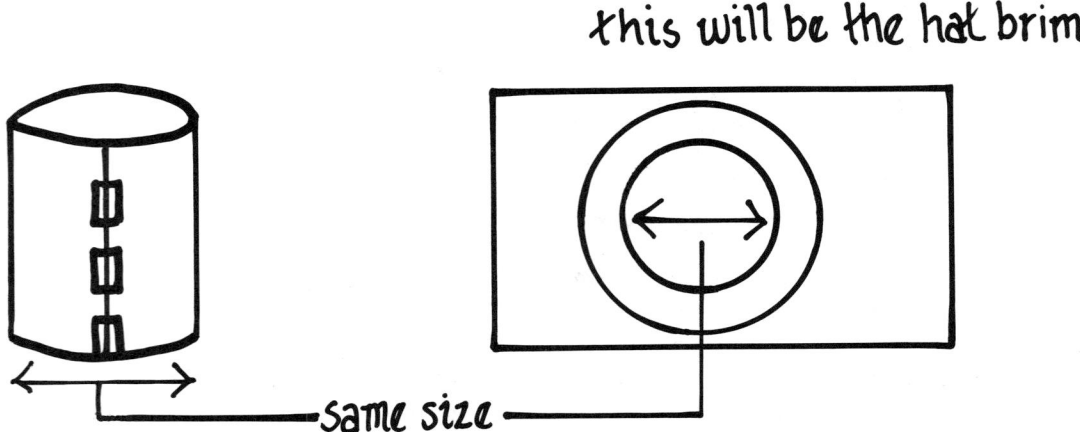

After the excess paper beyond the brim line is trimmed away, a cut is made into the interior of the circle and some material, in the shape of a circle is removed. What remains is notched to the head measurement line.

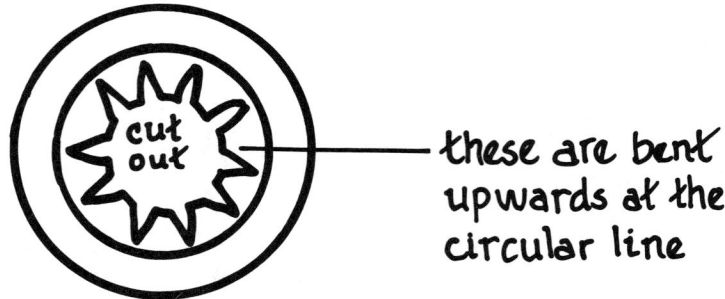

The tabs thus formed are bent upwards and pasted on the inner side of where a hat band would be at the base of the cylinder. Some strips of white paper are pasted over the red of the body of the hat, and voilà—a Cat in the Hat becomes imminent. It is not necessary to glue a circle over the open top, although I have done this in my more ambitious moments. A thin elastic pinned into the heavy overlap area to stretch under the child's chin makes for more carefree wearing of the hat for long intervals.

Putting the Costume Together

Although this construction may sound difficult, in actuality it is not. At an Erie School parade, this time in celebration of Dr. Seuss' 80th birthday, children of all ages were sporting this headgear, and I *know* that not all were made by parents.

The same pattern may be utilized, done in black, for the top hat, the signature of Abraham Lincoln. And, with a much lower crown, several hats may be made to stack on top of each other to make a respectable showing to represent the greater number carried on the head of the pedlar from *Caps for Sale*. At least the checked hat and one for each of the red, blue, brown, and gray caps would seem appropriate. For best balancing, a slight increase in size as the hats progress upwards is advisable. On the other hand, the audience always enjoys it if the pedlar's stack topples over. (The presence of a few monkeys to steal the hats would add to the fun.) Shortening the cylinder and using a paper towel to make a soft crown produces a hat that Christopher Columbus might wear, and so on.

I must insert, however, that after using teacher Betty Wilson's pattern for pedlar caps for *Caps for Sale*, I will no longer use the type with crown and brim. She cut pieces of construction paper to make the parts of a visor cap. Two staples simply and instantly produced completely satisfactory headgear.

Crowns for the royalty frequently occurring in literature for children are also simple to make. A piece of yellow construction paper, some glue, and a pair of scissors are the only materials required.

 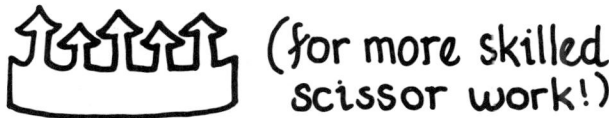

One *can* expect, however, that once a child gets a feeling of delight in being a princess or a king, he or she may want to attach costume jewelry to a heavier tagboard or cardboard crown.

Other head coverings may be created to fit the particular character. George Washington's tricorn hat will take this shape:

The comb of the Little Red Hen is readily fabricated.

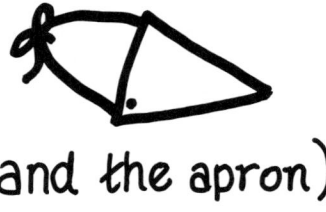

Rabbit ears, quickly made on the spur of the moment by an Erie teacher, Georgina Rico, ensured that a child was not disappointed at being excluded from a class-wide presentation of book characters to our kindergarteners.

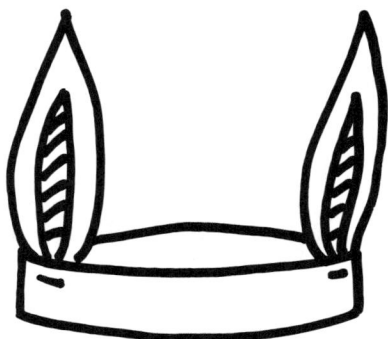

I have made a wire foundation from a clothes hanger for ears for Katy No-Pocket, the kangaroo, and pinned them on a cap of brown knit fabric that tied under my chin in a manner like that of a nylon stocking cap, but this effort *was* more challenging and time-consuming. In contrast, a very quick duck character head can be made by placing eyes above the visor on a visor cap.

Putting the Costume Together

Although headgear is usually of higher priority, bodies deserve some attention also. For inanimate objects, of course, costuming becomes the simplest yet. Children may be outfitted with sandwich boards or even just one-sided pieces of tagboard or cardboard. At my school one year, a marvelous creation of a Humpty Dumpty sitting on his wall was drawn on cardboard and merely suspended in front of the child. Once, our princess who slept on a pea was accompanied by another child covered by a huge, albeit flat, pea. One tip might be useful: Sandwich signs that fall below the knee make walking difficult.

At left is a slice of watermelon from *The Very Hungry Caterpillar*. Note: One of the circles represents the hole chewed by the caterpillar rather than another watermelon seed.

A basic body sack for young children can be made from a grocery sack or a shopping bag.

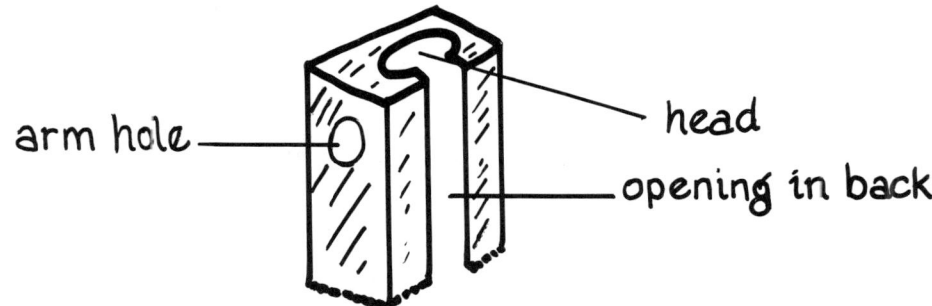

For taller children the sack may be lengthened by stapling paper cut from a second sack to the base of the first. For older (and wider) children a simple over-the-head tunic may be made with bulletin board paper.

This is a penguin body for Mr. Popper's Captain Cook.

A white blouse worn with a black jacket would do the trick for Captain Cook, also.

Although a bit more effort with paper body costumes produces a more finished look, my inclination, for purposes of the short term costumes for book characters is to keep the process as simple as possible. Still, perhaps in the case of the princess' pea, a more effective pea could have been made by gathering bulletin board paper, crepe paper, or fabric around the neck and legs and stuffing it to curve outward over the body, as Chernoff and Hartelius have so ably demonstrated with their "stuffed tomato."

Material measured double the distance from neck to knee

Fabric is stapled, wrong side out, holes left for arms

Leg holes are cut out of fold

Ribbon or string to gather the top

Putting the Costume Together

Although I have reiterated that I prefer working from the character to the costume, I must admit that a library club member's and my exact duplication of the snowman from the Chernoff and Hartelius title produced a wonderful Frosty the Snowman one year. (He did need a bit more stuffing.)

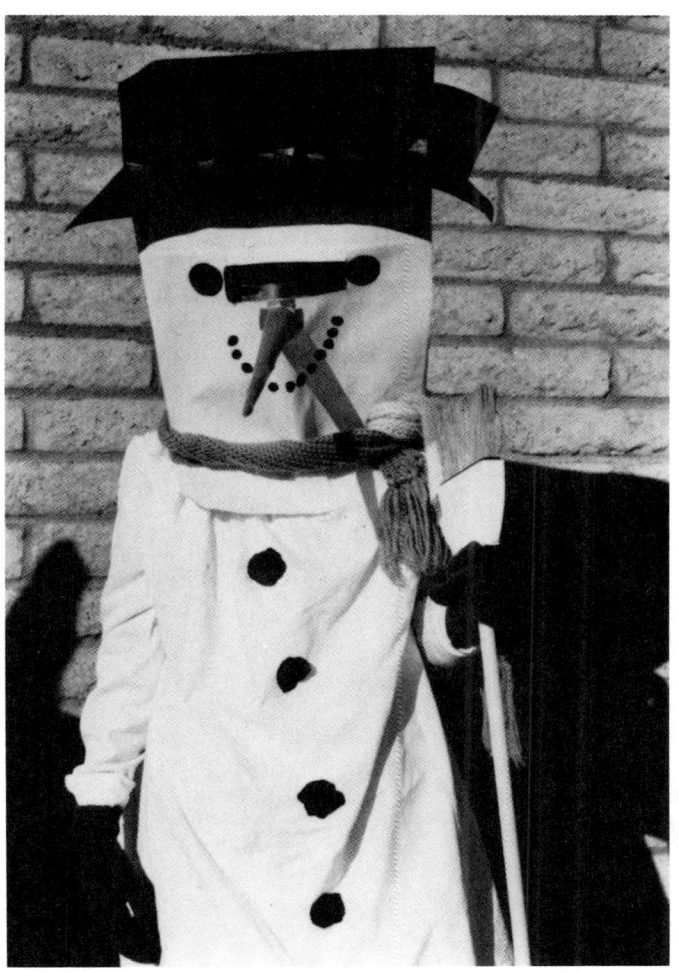

Frosty the Snowman

Recently, I discovered a way of dressing a character from head to toe with paper. Champlin and Renfro have named this kind of construction a bodi-puppet and give excellent directions for creating it in their *Storytelling with Puppets.*

Basically, the body is a paper sack and is tied around the neck by a string or ribbon. (The paper sack and costume itself covers only the front side of the body.) Three-inch wide strips of paper, or (even better in terms of ease of movement) fabric, are attached to the paper sack in the appropriate spots and are also attached to the child's limbs by means of a rubber band stapled into a cuff.

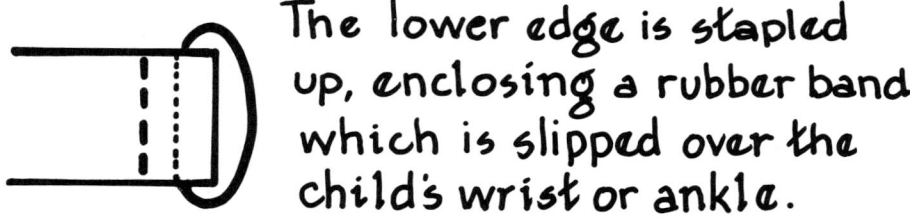

The character's head may be pasted on the flap of the grocery sack or a box headgear with the face attached may be added.

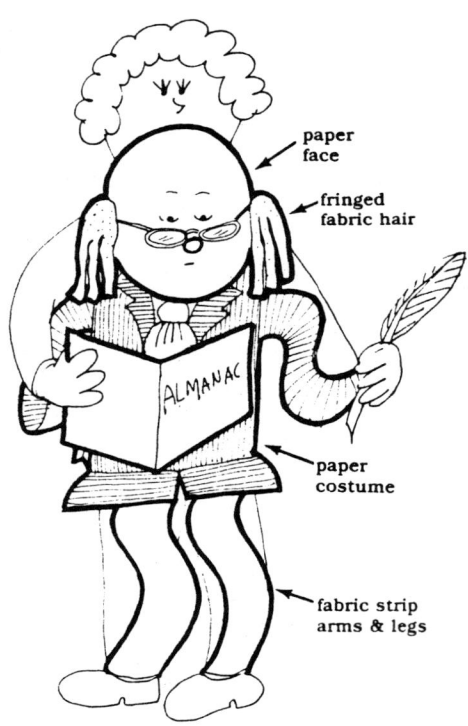

Ben Franklin bodi-puppet. Illustration reprinted by permission of the American Library Association from Connie Champlin and Nancy Renfro, *Storytelling with Puppets*, p. 51, copyright © 1985 by ALA.

Putting the Costume Together 31

Construction details and other examples of the bodi-puppet are also to be found in Nancy Renfro's *Bags Are Big! A Paper Bag Craft Book*.

Although it does not bother me in the least to have a four-legged animal walk on two legs for a parade, there are occasions when the general effect is improved by the use of two people for one animal, providing the necessary four legs.

Try a cereal box, for example, for a horse's snout. It would be spread into a circle shape at one end to make an opening to fit around the student's face. Knotted strings through each of two holes, made about a foot apart near the center of the short edge of a sheet will tie the "body" on around this first student's neck. The second student will climb under the sheet and bend over to produce a lumpfree back. He or she will hold onto the first student's waist for the most troublefree walking. Of course, *any* box headgear could be used with this body.

For Nancy Grubb's class presentation of *The Enormous Egg*, Uncle Beazley, the triceratops, was represented by two children in this fashion, with good results.

Heads and bodies are important but accessories may also make the costume. A few hints, given in head to toe order, are listed as follows:

Wig—may be a mop or a paper bag.

 (Curl the fringed ends around a pencil.)

Glasses—may be constructed from pipe cleaners.

Ears—if not placed on a mask, sack, or box, may be pinned on a sweatband or construction paper headband.

Make-up—One tablespoon soft shortening plus two tablespoons corn starch makes a base to which food coloring may be added for the appropriate color of skin.

Sugar and water solution will hold pieces of tissue (pink or yellow) which, after complete drying, may be wrinkled to produce the look of old age. Eye shadow for dark circles under the eyes will contribute to the effect. Vaseline provides a base for talcum powder for a chalky-white look.

Beard—Eisner's tips will prevent the slipping that I thought was inevitable.

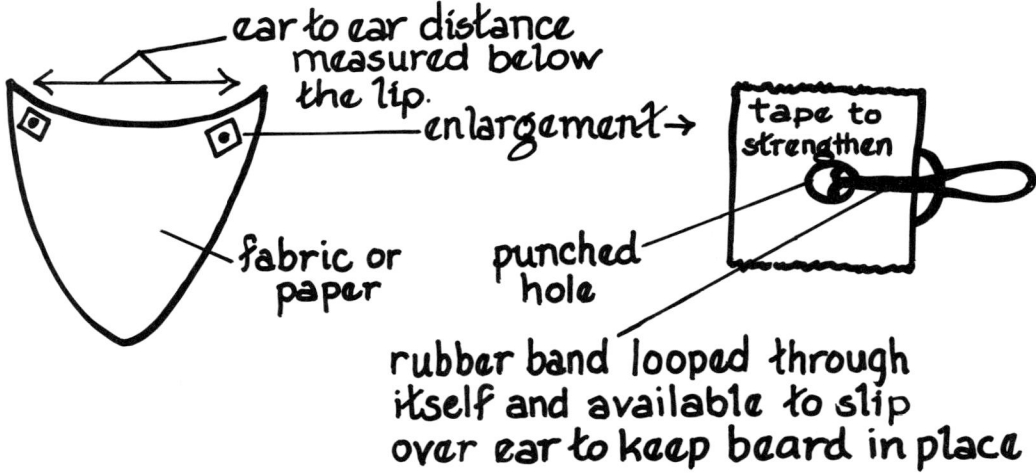

Wings—may be two more paper sacks over the arms or foil-covered wire suspended from the neck.

Sword—Cover cardboard with foil or silver wrapping paper.

Shield—for authentic positioning needs hand grip *and* arm holder. Tagboard loops will perform this service. However, just the lid of a garbage can would suit my purposes.

Tail—is not essential. They do add that final touch to the character, however, and kids love them. Crepe or construction paper will do the trick or a length of thick rope may be used. My long trailing kangaroo tail was cut from brown bulletin board paper. For my permanent prop box I made a lengthy tube from black fabric and stuffed it with cotton in readiness for my next Cat in the Hat master of ceremonies. Haley (see page 37) is the best costume book source for tail construction.

Feet—may be tagboard or paper plates, taped at the back of the ankle. However, my recommendation is to avoid these additions in parade situations.

Signs—Three words are necessary about the lettering on signs to ensure that they may be read from a distance. (See page 33.)

LARGE

DARK

LEGIBLE

The listings that follow may be of assistance in locating a character when the costume, in idea form or in actuality, has been selected first. (Page references for ideas for representing many of these characters, along with some additional ones, will be found under the headings "bear," "cat," "dog," etc. in the Character Index.)

Bear Costume
Blackboard Bear from titles by Alexander
Little Bear from *Sand Cake* and *Just Like Daddy* (Asch)
Sam from *Popcorn* (Asch)
Berenstain bears from numerous titles by Stan and Jan Berenstain
Paddington Bear from Bond titles
Joe from *How Joe the Bear and Sam the Mouse Got Together* (De Regniers)
Mr. Bear from *Ask Mr. Bear* (Flack)
Corduroy, Beady Bear and Bearymore from Don Freeman titles
Bear from *Hound and Bear* (Gackenbach)
Grizzwold from the Hoff title of the same name
Little Bear from *Little Bear's Thanksgiving* and other titles by Janice
Big Bear from titles by Margolis
Winnie-the-Pooh from A. A. Milne titles
Little Bear from *A Kiss for Little Bear* and other titles by Minarik
Jason Bear from *I'm Terrific* (Sharmat)
Biggest Bear from the Ward title of the same name
Boris from the Boris and Morris series (Wiseman)

Cat Costume
Herman from the Georgie series by Robert Bright
Chester from *Bunnicula* and other titles by James Howe
"The Three Little Kittens" (Mother Goose)
Harry Cat from *The Cricket in Times Square* and other titles by George Selden
Cat in the Hat in titles by Dr. Seuss

Dog Costume
Clifford, the Big Red Dog from titles by Bridwell
Ribsy in *Henry Huggins* and other titles by Cleary
Claude from *Claude the Dog* or *Claude and Pepper* (Gackenbach)
Hound from *Hound and Bear* and its sequel (Gackenbach)
Harold from *Bunnicula* and other titles by Howe
Diggingest Dog (Perkins)
Huppy from *Harry Cat's Pet Puppy* (Selden)
Harry the Dirty Dog from titles by Zion
(No mention needs to be made of Snoopy)

Lion Costume
King Lion from *Why Mosquitoes Buzz in People's Ears* (Aardema)
Happy Lion from Fatio titles

Putting the Costume Together

Johnny Lion from titles by Hurd
Aslan from *The Lion, the Witch, and the Wardrobe* (Lewis)

Mouse Costume
Ralph from *The Mouse and the Motorcycle, Runaway Ralph* or *Ralph S. Mouse* (Cleary)
Sam from *How Joe the Bear and Sam the Mouse Got Together* (DeRegniers)
O Crispin from *The Champion of Merrimack County* (Drury)
Squeaky from Janice titles, e.g. *Little Bear Marches in the St. Patrick's Day Parade*
baby mouse from *Mother, Mother, I Want Another* (Polushkin)
Abel from *Abel's Island* (Steig)
Anatole from various Titus titles
Miss Rosa Burrow-Minder from *Mice on Ice* (Yolen)
(I would choose not to include Mickey Mouse, except in combination with a representation of Walt Disney.)

See Dogs—Fiction, and Mice—Fiction (or —Stories, in older libraries) and so on in your own card catalog for many additional characters to fit particular costumes. See also pages 9 to 13 for listings of ghost, rabbit, and witch character ideas.

Once again, those props which point out the distinctiveness of the character cannot be overemphasized. For example, Little Bear from *Little Bear Marches in the St. Patrick's Day Parade* would carry an opened umbrella and have a stuffed mouse, Squeaky, on his shoulder; the Biggest Bear might be pretending to drink jugs of maple syrup or eating a piece of maple sugar removed from a box clearly marked, "Maple Sugar"; Winnie-the-Pooh might have a blue balloon in his hand or a pot labelled "Huny" and a pitcher marked "Condensed Milk"; Corduroy, of course, would wear corduroy overalls and would perhaps be looking in a laundry bag, calling out, "Where's a pocket for me?"

Many books on making costumes are available. Pattern books, such as *Simplicity* and *McCall's*, also are sources for instructions for costume-making which would have to be undertaken by a parent. Our parades at Erie have always included a sprinkling of these, but I really feel that many of the benefits of the process for the child, including the joy from developing his or her own ideas, are bypassed with the use of such pattern books.

In a similar vein, I appreciate costume books that encourage children's choices and give ideas for variations in preference to those that give minute, step-by-step directions for a particular costume. However, I realize there must be a market for both.

The following bibliography lists all the children's costume books that I have had a chance to explore. It is not an inclusive list. For the teacher or parent just getting started with book character costuming I would highly recommend that the Chernoff title be consulted first. For stressing creativity and for providing the most detail for accessory-making, perhaps for more professional results than I am interested in for book characters, the Haley title is superb. For a book that is not basically designed for costuming ideas but that illustrates many stick puppets (which can be translated into masks) and that also gives ideas for dramatizations appropriate for children as book characters as well as for puppets, turn to Connie Champlin and Nancy Renfro's *Storytelling with Puppets* (American Library Association 1985).

Happy costuming.

Bibliography of Children's Costume Books

Boyers, Janet, *Making Paper Costumes*. Plays, Inc., 1974.

Instructions for making, decorating and fireproofing paper costumes. Includes a short section on using paper sack body covers for seven- to nine-year-olds, but a major portion of the book shows details and diagrams of paper linking for elaborate costumes, most of which are suited for ages beyond elementary school.

Chernoff, Goldie, and Margaret Hartelius, *Easy Costumes You Don't Have to Sew*. Four Winds, 1975.

Using the basic sack, paper bags, sandwich boards, garbage bags, and cartons, Chernoff and Hartelius clearly show how to create a marvelous array of visually effective costumes with no sewing required. Costumes range from tomatoes to dragons. Sketches and diagrams communicate well. Final sections on hats, pleated paper uses, and quick disguises, as well as the "mix and match" ideas are excellent, also.

Cox, Marcia, *Creature Costumes*. Grosset and Dunlap, 1977.

This title basically focuses on headgear for monsters and outer space entities. Precise diagrams, clear step-by-step directions, and helpful photos of each stage of construction are given.

Eisner, Vivienne, *Quick and Easy Holiday Costumes*. Lothrop, Lee, & Shepard, 1977.

After focusing on five basic costumes, the author goes month-by-month through the year, offering "more than 5 dozen costumes for 23 (special) days, all made with inexpensive and easily available tools and materials." Includes a cuckoo clock for New Year's; Mother Nature for Earth and Arbor Day; a dreydl for Chanukah; and various historical figures. No sewing is required and encouragement is given to mix and match to create costumes of one's own design.

Gates, Frieda, *Easy to Make Costumes*. Harvey House, 1978.

Very specific directions as to materials and tools, and step-by-step, relatively large print instructions are given for making costumes from sheets, boxes, paper, plastic bags, old clothes, and fabric. Diagrams are simple and effective, and some individual creativity is encouraged.

Gates, Frieda, *Easy to Make Monster Masks and Disguises*. Harvey House, 1979.

In this title over 20 different ways of making masks and head covers are shown. Materials include a variety of items available in the household, including bleach bottles and foil. No sewing is required. The written directions are tied in to the diagrams and allow some individual variations. Suggestions for partial mask disguises and disguise headwear would be helpful for book characters.

Gilbreath, Alice, *Making Costumes for Parties, Plays, and Holidays*. Morrow, 1974.

This is a straightforward listing of materials, tools, and steps for making 21 costumes, ranging from ghost, through record player and grandfather clock, to frog and dragon. Wire, fabric, paper, cardboard, and boxes are utilized. The specific directions do not call for creativity but they are very easy to understand. Simple sewing is required.

Putting the Costume Together

Glovach, Linda, *The Little Witch's Black Magic Book of Disguises*. Prentice-Hall, 1973.

This book includes "directions for making such disguises as Peter Pan, Alice in Wonderland, a ski accident and various holiday costumes requiring inexpensive materials and no sewing." Directions are given conversationally and improvising is encouraged.

Haley, Gail, *Costumes for Plays and Playing*. Methuen, 1978.

This title stresses creativity on the part of the costume-maker and the use of treasure box materials. It also shows how to cut patterns, drape bodies, apply make-up, and construct such accessories as helmets, shields, shoe buckles, and mermaids' tails. It is filled with helpful sketches.

Leedy, Loreen, *The Dragon Halloween Party* (A Story and Activity Book.) Holiday House, 1986.

Included in this picture story book along with its rhymed account of a dragon family's Halloween party are instructions for food, decorations, *and* a dozen costumes. Whimsical dragons are charmingly combined with straightforward directions which should work nicely, as long as safety pins and/or tape are substituted for the glue suggested for attaching "ribbons."

Renfro, Nancy, *Bags Are Big! A Paper Bag Craft Book*. Nancy Renfro Studios, 1986.

The craft techniques in this book, which is illustrated with excellent photographs and diagrams, certainly could be adapted for costuming. "Beastly Bags," "Bionic Bag Friends," and "Bodi-Bag Super Stars" provide specific help for basic headgear and body coverings.

IV. IDEAS FOR CHARACTERS FROM MOTHER GOOSE

NO OTHER GENRE OF CHILDREN'S literature has as many uniquely vivid characters, just begging to be portrayed, as Mother Goose. And, because the rhymes are *almost* as universally known as the creations of the mass media, the presence of Mother Goose characters in a children's book celebration ensures that the audience will experience the joy of identification.

You may think that your upper grade students are too sophisticated or "cool" to dress up as these characters. Not so. An appeal for the portrayal of some Mother Goose characters so that the kindergartners would be able to recognize and enjoy them will bring volunteers in sufficient number.

You and your students will have your own remembered favorites from early childhood. They may or may not be included in the following short list:

CHARACTER/RHYME	COSTUME, PROP, ACTION, PARTNER IDEAS
BABY from "Rock-a-Bye Baby"	Doll in cradle; child dressed as tree (body as trunk, branches anchored on box headgear, with leaves attached to branches and to child's arms.) Child would rock cradle in arms. An alternate idea for the tree would be to merely drape a swatch of sheer green fabric over the child's head and torso, a quick representation that I have used frequently for simple dramatizations of Ets' *Play with Me*.
BLACK SHEEP from "Baa, Baa, Black Sheep"	Sheep headgear; black clothing for body. Accompanied by boy holding a bag labelled "sheep wool." The sheep could carry two other bags.
CAT from "Hey Diddle, Diddle"	Cat headgear on child who would hold a violin in his or her hand. Could be accompanied by student in cow headgear, jumping over a model of a crescent moon; one in dog headgear, the dog's face in a laugh and the student echoing the laugh with body movements; and one in sandwich board dish with a large model of a spoon attached.
CROOKED MAN from "There Was a Crooked Man"	Hunched over figure, dressed in men's clothing, one hand holding his back, the other grasping a crooked staff. Should include another student wearing a tagboard or cardboard cutout of a crooked house.

Clockwise, from top left: Humpty Dumpty; Little Miss Muffet; Mary, Mary Quite Contrary; Little Bo Peep.

CHARACTER/RHYME	COSTUME, PROP, ACTION, PARTNER IDEAS
HUMPTY DUMPTY	Large piece of cardboard designed as stone wall, topped by a cardboard egg with features and clothes drawn in, attached around student's neck. Egg could be pasted on box headgear.
JACK AND JILL	Ordinary clothes for boy and girl; pail to hold between them; bandaged head for Jack as well as gestures of pain relating to his head injury. (Try the school nurse for an Ace bandage.) Erie students applied exaggerated freckles and rosy cheeks and delighted the kindergartners by pantomiming the pumping and the fall.
JACK from "Jack Be Nimble"	Student in robe and stocking cap with candle in low candle holder in hand. Would place the candle on the ground and leap over it.
LITTLE BO PEEP	Long dress; bonnet; shepherd's crook; stuffed lamb under arm; worried expression as she raises her hand to her forehead to scan the horizon for sheep. (The crook could be a sawed-off broom handle, dowel, or narrow length of wood extended into a curve by the use of tagboard wrapped with masking tape. The end result can be beautified by the addition of a layer of streamer crepe paper.) Another student in sheep headgear could be peeking from a hiding place unnoticed by Little Bo Peep.
LITTLE BOY BLUE	Blue clothing; horn; straw in hair; sleepy demeanor, rubbing eyes.
LITTLE MISS MUFFET	Peasant dress; bowl and spoon in hands. Student would have to be running, expressing fright, from an accompanying spider.
MARY from "Mary Had a Little Lamb"	This character is one that is likely to be confused with Little Bo Peep by audiences. She may be easily differentiated, however, if she carries, in addition to the lamb, a slate, and/or a lunch pail.
MARY from "Mary, Mary Quite Contrary"	Long dress; wide-brimmed hat trimmed with flowers; watering can; hoe, and/or a few paper flowers for the other hand. Could be accompanied by several children with flower face masks in single line.
MOUSE from "Hickory, Dickory Dock"	Mouse headgear. Would have to be joined by another child wearing a grandfather clock, the hands of which should point to one o'clock.

Characters from Mother Goose

CHARACTER/RHYME	COSTUME, PROP, ACTION, PARTNER IDEAS
OLD KING COLE	Long robe; crown; pipe; bowl; laughing demeanor. Should be accompanied by three students, ideally dressed alike, each with a fiddle, either real or flat homemade variety.
OLD WOMAN from "There Was an Old Woman Who Lived in a Shoe"	Child with babushka and long skirt with large soup pot, offering large spoonful of its pretend contents to many, preferably smaller, children. She could also carry a thin tree branch with which to whip her children. A large backdrop of a shoe would provide the finishing touch.
PETER from "Peter, Peter, Pumpkin Eater"	Boy with spoon and scooped out pumpkin. Could be accompanied by a second student wearing a depiction of the wife in a pumpkin shell anchored on a sandwich board base.
QUEEN OF HEARTS	Long dress; crown; train; tart tin with tarts or tagboard model of same; red construction paper hearts on crown and other items of clothing. Could be joined by the knave of hearts (a sandwich board jack of hearts would do) who would steal the tarts.
THREE LITTLE KITTENS	Three students in cat headgear each holding up a pair of mittens and exhibiting happy behavior. Or, the three could be crying, rubbing their eyes, emitting vigorous sobbing mews as a fourth, larger child/cat, as mother, shakes her finger at them scolding them about the loss of their mittens.

I am sure that you and your students will enjoy thinking out your own representations. I wish good luck to you and your Mother Goose aficionados.

V. IDEAS FOR CHARACTERS FROM FABLES AND FOLK AND FAIRY TALES

PROBABLY SECOND ONLY TO Mother Goose in being peopled with well-known and colorful characters are the folk and fairy tales. As with Mother Goose representations, it is always good to include at least a few of the characters from the old familiar tales in a celebration for universal recognition and appeal and for the special enjoyment of the younger members of the audience.

My partial list may leave out some of your favorites, but I wager that you and your students will be quite capable of plotting out a costume for some unmentioned hero, now that you have the pattern.

Do encourage brain storming by the class or in small groups, and do realize that the first idea might not be the best. I am reminded of one second grade class that produced five Cinderellas ready for the ball for one book celebration event. Each little girl thought it wonderful to parade in her best and fanciest long dress. I think, however, that both the participants and the audience would have gained if the teacher had taken a little time to explore other possibilities. As a welcome relief from all this pulchritude, another Cinderella entry by a fourth grader in the same parade was delightful. This student chose to be a bedraggled, work-ridden Cinderella. She dressed herself in a patchwork of tattered clothing, including a headkerchief, and carried a pail and a scrubbing brush. Of course, her face and clothing were appropriately smeared with "cinders."

I am sure that you can, similarly, improve on some of the ideas that follow.

CHARACTER/TITLE	COSTUME, PROP, ACTION, PARTNER IDEAS
BREMEN TOWN MUSICIANS	Donkey, dog, cat, and rooster headgear or masks. They could be walking along by themselves, carrying a sign "To Bremen Town" and "singing." Or, they could be preceded by four students dressed as robbers, running in fear, knives and forks still in their hands. For a class production the inclusion of the masters and mistresses of the four musicians would allow more students to participate, e.g., the rooster would be chased by the farm woman with her hatchet raised.
CINDERELLA	Long dress; tiara perhaps; definitely one shoe in hand or lost immediately in front of the audience. (Alternate version is described in the introduction to this chapter, above.) Could be accompanied by the prince, with a shoe in his hand or the fairy godmother with her wand and perhaps a pumpkin in hand. The stepmother and/or the ugly stepsisters could also be added, scowling and shaking their fingers at Cinderella.

 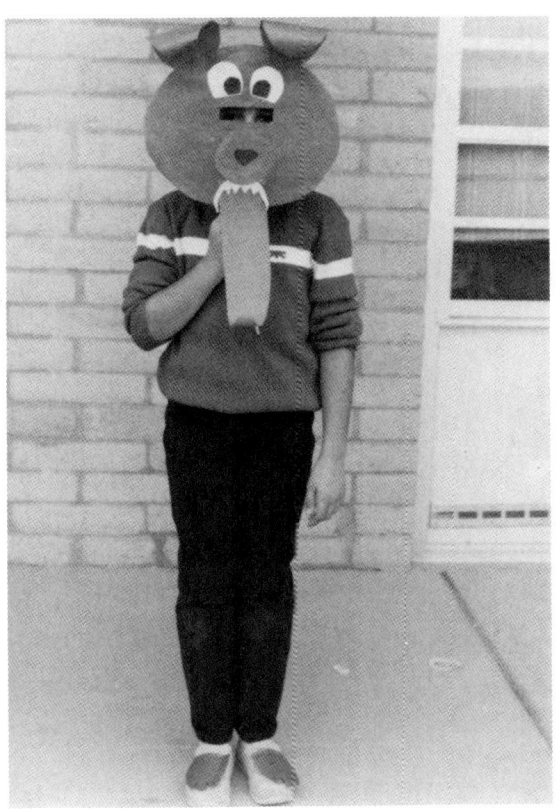

Top left: Two of The Three Little Pigs; *right:* The Wolf; *bottom:* Snow White.

CHARACTER/TITLE	COSTUME, PROP, ACTION, PARTNER IDEAS
COUNTRY MOUSE AND THE CITY MOUSE	Mouse headgear or mask. The one would be fitted with a straw hat and the student would wear worn jeans or overalls, plaid shirt, and have hay sticking out of his or her pockets and hat. The city mouse would wear a top hat and a suit and assume a regal, snobbish bearing, perhaps using the thumbs-in-armholes gesture of pride. Both could run at the sight of a dog.
GINGERBREAD MAN	Girl with long dress and cap, made up to appear old; cookie sheet with large gingerbread man, either authentic or made of construction paper, on it. An alternate idea would be to have a child wearing a body-size shape of the gingerbread man running away from the old woman who would indicate her displeasure by shaking her hands and arms at him or her. Could be chased also by a cow, a pig, and two farmers, as well as the "little old man."
GOLDILOCKS	Peasant-type blouse or dress; spoon; bowl; or pieces of broken chair. (One year our custodian took a student chair apart for us.) Could be running away from the group of three bears.
HANSEL AND GRETEL	Shorts with tagboard braces to simulate lederhosen for Hansel; peasant blouse and dirndl skirt for Gretel. Or, just ragged clothing befitting a poverty-stricken family, typified by exaggerated saw-toothed edges on the children's clothing. Props might include smooth white stones to be dropped or a loaf of unsliced bread to shred into crumbs. A mock-up of the gingerbread house could be worn by another child. A witch with a luscious piece of candy in her hand might be beckoning to the children.
HARE AND TORTOISE	A rabbit costume would be worn by a student who might be running vigorously in place with a horror-struck expression on his or her face (or mask). A second student, with a "shell" constructed from a round or oval shaped laundry basket, could be crawling on hands and knees. Or, an upright tortoise, dressed in round sandwich boards and headgear decorated with scales, could be inching along on two feet instead. A string held by two additional students could be labelled "finish line" and the tortoise and these two students would cheer as the line is crossed.
JACK AND THE BEANSTALK	Boy in regular clothing could carry any of the following: hatchet, hen, bag of gold (with a label to commu-

Characters from Fables

CHARACTER/TITLE	COSTUME, PROP, ACTION, PARTNER IDEAS
	nicate), replica of a golden harp, or beanstalk (a broomstick, wrapped with green crepe paper and festooned with leaves). Jack may be accompanied by a child dressed as a beanpole, one as the hen clutching her golden egg, or a giant. The child portraying the giant does not have to be very large since a huge head as a stick puppet mask does the job well.
KING MIDAS	Long robe; crown; apple, red on one side, gold on the other, or plate covered with gold wrapping paper holding some recognizable food colored a golden color. The king would have an expression of panic on his face.
LION from Aesop's "The Lion and the Mouse"	Animal headgear for both lion and the mouse. Lion could be tied up by a net of ropes and be roaring or the mouse could be holding the frayed end of a rope triumphantly with the lion thanking him.
LITTLE RED HEN	Red clothing and comb (see page 26) or bird headgear; apron; hoe or white sack labelled "flour." Could be accompanied by mouse, dog, and cat (Galdone's version), each saying, "Not I!" Or the red hen could be serving bread or cake to a number of chicks.
LITTLE RED RIDING HOOD	Red cape with hood, either fabric or paper; basket with handle and cloth napkin to cover contents; screams of "Help!! Save me from the wolf!" while running. A wolf might follow her and grandma in her nightgown and nightcap might be running with her. A woodsman, with ax outstretched, might follow the wolf.
MOTHER HOLLY (Galdone book of the same name)	Long dress; enlarged front teeth; comforter held in hand. May be accompanied by one child with a pot of gold and one, with smudged face, covered with "tar" (pinned on pieces of black bulletin board paper).
OLD WOMAN AND HER PIG	Long dress; bonnet; aged face (see page 32); bent over posture; walking stick. Should be accompanied by at least one child in pig headgear. A stuffed pig might suffice.
PAUL BUNYAN	Headgear with Paul's face extending over the edges, making it "larger than life." Similar headgear for Babe, the blue ox. Paul would carry an ax and might take big steps across a large map of the United States.

CHARACTER/TITLE	COSTUME, PROP, ACTION, PARTNER IDEAS
PRINCESS AND THE PEA	Tiara; train (lace slip or curtain); pillow on which rests a ball of green yarn.
PUSS IN BOOTS	Cat headgear; rubber boots; fishing pole and large fish (cardboard).
ROBIN HOOD	Cape and tights, preferably green; bag of money. Cap as shown: 
SNOW WHITE AND DWARVES	Long dress; apple, real or giant-sized tagboard one, with missing bite. Students have really enjoyed depicting Disney's dwarves; e.g., Sleepy has appeared in night shirt and nightcap, clutching a pillow and yawning.
THREE BILLY GOATS GRUFF	Face masks which include horns and beards for three children who correspond in size to the three goats. Troll mask probably is readily available in some commercial monster format, but, as you might expect, my bias is for the creation of a long-nosed, hideous face as an art assignment. An added touch might be a cardboard bridge (or a couple of classroom chairs tied together) for the troll to hold over his head and peer out from under.
THREE LITTLE PIGS AND WOLF	Face masks; props of straw, either real or drawn on tagboard, colored, and, if necessary for communication, labelled; pieces of lumber; and bricks. Wheelbarrels would be a great addition. Completed houses made of cardboard and worn or carried by other children would be a nice addition, and, of course, the wolf should be present, huffing and puffing endlessly.

Characters from Fables

CHARACTER/TITLE	COSTUME, PROP, ACTION, PARTNER IDEAS
WIND AND THE SUN	Very large stick masks or box headgear with the shapes extending beyond the boxes, the one of a cloud shape, with eyes and mouth drawn in and an extension suggesting the air being blown, the second of a sun, again with a face. The wind could use his or her body to emphasize the blowing, much like the wolf's huffing and puffing. A third person, dressed as the traveller in a cloak would respond to the wind by shivering and drawing his cloak up tightly. As the sun would take its turn, the traveller would remove his cloak and mop his brow in response to the warmth. For a class production designed to utilize more students, the ships tossing in the harbor from the wind's efforts and the flowers blooming and bees buzzing in response to the sun could also be portrayed.

WOODCUTTER from "The Three Wishes"	Jeans; plaid shirt; ax. Face mask with long nose projecting from it on which is suspended a sausage. Could be accompanied by a wife, in a long dress and cap, voicing her complaints at him. (Note: Some versions of the story have the sausage attached to the wife.)

VI. IDEAS FOR CHARACTERS FROM PICTURE STORY BOOKS AND READERS

THERE ARE SO MANY LOVEABLE personalities found in picture books that it seems difficult to choose some favorites. As a librarian who enjoys reading to classes, I have relished positive response and indications of feelings of real endearment from children towards many of the fantasized but truly believable characters in children's picture story books. To name but a few of the examples that come to mind readily: Kindergartners have received special pleasure from the stories about Alfie, the gunniwolf, the wild baby, Curious George, and Harry the dirty dog, and have worn out many copies of *The Chalk Box Story*; first graders have claimed Marc Brown's Arthur, Corduroy, the baby mouse from *Mother, Mother, I Want Another*, and Danny and his dinosaur as their own; second graders have appreciated the humor of Gackenbach's *Hound and Bear*, Du Bois' *Lazy Tommy Pumpkinhead*, and Marshall's *George and Martha*, and so on.

I would make my first choices for characters to be represented at my school from the above. Your choices would rightfully be made according to the picture story books that you have found to have "clicked" at your own school.

Of course, if the following listing introduces some new characters that you and your students enjoy, more the better. Do bear in mind that for series books, as mentioned previously in relation to delineating characters from longer fiction, one incident or situation should be focused on in choosing props for the best communication of the character.

CHARACTER	AUTHOR AND TITLE(S)	COSTUME, PROP, ACTION, PARTNER IDEAS
ALEXANDER	*Alexander Who Used to Be Rich Last Sunday*	School clothing; half melted candle in holder; Teddy bear with one eye; deck of cards; sign stating "Toys for Rent."
	Alexander and the Terrible, Horrible, No Good, Very Bad Day (Viorst)	One of the calamities would be represented, such as the gum in the hair or the dripping sweater or Alexander could be captured simply with a student, face in a scowl, carrying a sign, "I am going to Australia!" For a class effort, Alexander, assisted by brothers with toys and cereal boxes in hand and a storelady who would say, "We're out of your size" for example, would detail several of the problems. The class would join in chorus with the "It was a terrible, horrible . . ." after each complaint.
ALFIE	*Alfie Gets in First*	Short pants; basket of groceries; stool. Could be joined by the mother and a crying Mary Rose in a stroller or a window washer with a ladder.

 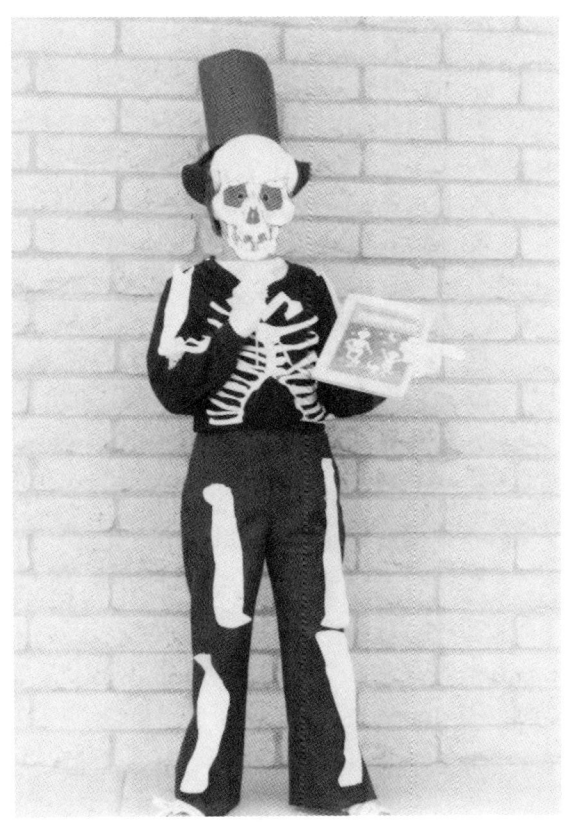
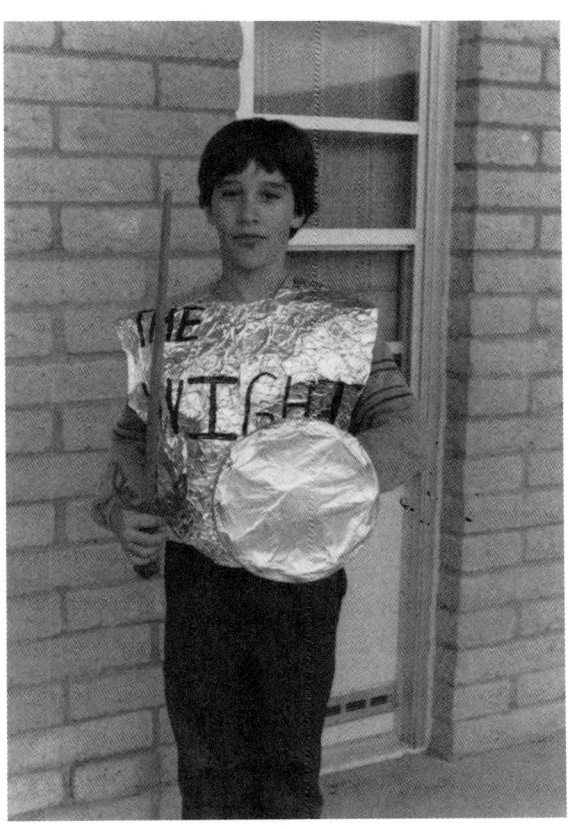 

Top: Skeletons from *Funnybones; bottom:* De Paola's *The Knight and the Dragon.*

Clockwise from top left: Strega Nona and Big Anthony, from De Paola's *Strega Nona*; The Cat in the Hat; Little Rabbit (Who Wanted Red Wings); Clifford, from Bridwell's series.

The funny little woman and two wicked *oni*, from Mosel's *The Funny Little Woman*.

Curious George, the man with the big yellow hat, and assorted hospital personnel from *Curious George Goes to the Hospital*.

CHARACTER	AUTHOR AND TITLE(S)	COSTUME, PROP, ACTION, PARTNER IDEAS
	Alfie's Feet	Yellow boots, conspicuously marked L and R. Alfie would be stomping through a "puddle"—a piece of blue bulletin board paper.
	Also, *Alfie Gives a Hand* (Hughes)	
AMELIA BEDELIA	*Amelia Bedelia* *Come Back, Amelia Bedelia* *Good Work, Amelia Bedelia* *Play Ball, Amelia Bedelia* *Teach Us, Amelia Bedelia* and other titles, all beginning, *Amelia Bedelia . . .* (Parish)	Dress, preferably dark; white apron; hat with flowers; purse over arm. Props depend on title and incident selected. Could be light bulbs and clothespins, a sketch pad with "drawn" drapes, or a chicken dressed in baby clothing for the original title. A bat and a stolen second base, the latter labelled as such, would represent *Play Ball, Amelia Bedelia*. Of course, Amelia Bedelia would have to wear a marching band type uniform for this title.
ANATOLE	*Anatole* and many other titles, all beginning with *Anatole and . . .* (Titus)	Mouse headgear. A large trayful of various cheeses could be carried, each with Anatole's comment on a sign attached to a popsicle stick and stuck into the cheese. The cheese could be made of pieces of styrofoam, painted orange and cream.
ARTHUR	*Arthur's Nose* *Arthur's Eyes* *Arthur's Valentine* *Arthur's Halloween* *Arthur's Thanksgiving*, etc. (Marc Brown)	Face mask or box headgear. Props dependent on title: valentines and giant Hershey's kiss for *Arthur's Valentine;* Superman costume (cape and homemade "S" for a plain T-shirt) for *Arthur's Halloween*.
ARTHUR	*Arthur's Halloween Costume* *Arthur's Christmas Cookies* *Arthur's Honey Bear* *Arthur's Pen Pal* *Arthur's Prize Reader* (Lillian Hoban)	For Arthur's appearance from *Arthur's Halloween Costume* the following would do the trick: a sheet, splotched with red for the ketchup Arthur spilled, draped over the child's shoulders; a piece of shaggy brown material for the head; a garbage can lid, a broom, and the head of a doll in hand. A stuffed or cardboard black cat attached to the "wig" would be the crowning touch for Arthur's "The Spirit of Halloween" costume. Violet, carrying her trick and treat bag and costumed with crown, wand, wings, and long nightgown as the fairy queen, could attend him. It would be fun, also, to replicate the chocolate kiss costume

Characters from Picture Story Books

CHARACTER	AUTHOR AND TITLE(S)	COSTUME, PROP, ACTION, PARTNER IDEAS
		shown for Wilma's cousin Peter. Box or bag headgear could be used but they would not be as necessary for Arthur as for other animals because of the humanoid characteristics of the chimpanzee.
ARTHUR	*An Anteater Named Arthur* (Waber)	Cap; mask or box headgear with long nose. Focus on single episode for props; e.g., "Sometimes Arthur forgets things" represented by Arthur carrying sneakers, pencil case, spelling book, and a sign saying "I didn't forget my good-bye kiss"; or bestowing a kiss on an accompanying mother anteater, wearing a long dress, apron, and cap. The bushy tails can be created with a spiral of partially unravelled burlap.
BABY BEAR	*Just Like Daddy*	Bear headgear; fishing pole; boots. Should be imitating Papa Bear in picking flower for presenting to Mama Bear, for example. The fish could be made from cardboard or papier-mâché, and, naturally Mama would have the largest one and Papa, a shrimp of a fish.
	Sand Cake (Asch)	Bathing suits; sand pail and shovel. Baby Bear could be showing a picture of himself with the "eaten" cake in his stomach, or holding a plate with a real sand cake on it, or be eating authentic cake offered by his mother from a picnic basket.

BABY MOUSE	*Mother, Mother, I Want Another* (Polushkin)	Mouse headgear; pajamas; toothbrush or drink of water in hand. Would be rubbing eyes and sobbing. Could be joined by Mother Mouse with a bedtime story in hand. A float/wagon/bed could be made for baby mouse and the title would make a good small group production with all the other characters represented:
		    Mrs. Duck—offering worms
		    Mrs. Frog—offering flies
		    Mrs. Pig—with carrots in hand
		    Mrs. Donkey—with songbook, singing a lullabye.
		 To all offers, of course, Baby Mouse would shout out a high-pitched "No!" After the final, "I want another bedtime kiss!" all the animals would oblige.

BEA	*Bea and Mr. Jones* (Schwartz)	Girl in man's suit and tie; hair pulled back in side barrettes; briefcase. She could chant

CHARACTER	AUTHOR AND TITLE(S)	COSTUME, PROP, ACTION, PARTNER IDEAS
		her jingle about Crumby Crackers. Could be joined by a bald man wearing glasses, shirt and sweater, trousers, ideally with a large check pattern, and sneakers. He could be turning cartwheels or carrying an oversize "Dear Miss Seymour" note.
BENJAMIN	*Pumpernickle Tickle and Mean Green Cheese*	Benjamin in school clothes. Box headgear with extended trunk for El who would have to join him. Between them they could carry a loaf of bread, a piece of yellow cheese, and a dill pickle (exaggerated oversize one, please) and be engaging in nonsensical word play. They could, for example, say, "Dark brown belly-tickle, and a half-pound bumper stickle" in a chant together and pretend to double over with laughter.
	Nobody Knows I Have Delicate Toes (Patz)	For this title Benjamin would wear pajamas and El would carry a bath towel and soap.
BERENSTAIN BEARS	Many titles, most beginning, *The Bears'* . . . or *The Berenstain Bears and . . .*	Bear headgear. Props depend on title and incident selected. For the *Bears' Christmas*, for example, Papa Bear would appear with skis or toboggan. Mama Bear with her hat covered with garbage would be an amusing choice from *The Bears' Vacation*. Representation of either of the above-mentioned titles could include some smaller children in bear headgear for portrayal of all family members.
	Bears in the Night (Stan and Jan Berenstain)	Could be illustrated simply with one bear, in face mask, carrying a paper lantern. Might be attended by a child wearing a black head cover and wings, and emitting a loud "Whooo" as the owl.

BIG ANTHONY	*Strega Nona* *Big Anthony and the Magic Ring*	Hat; trousers and smock, large enough to accommodate a pillow stomach; fork; bowl heaped with spaghetti (false bottom of paper using minimal amount of pasta on top);

Characters from Picture Story Books

CHARACTER	AUTHOR AND TITLE(S)	COSTUME, PROP, ACTION, PARTNER IDEAS
	Strega Nona's Magic Lessons (De Paola)	attitude of nauseated pain, grabbing stomach. Could be joined by Strega Nona in a long skirt, apron, and babushka, carrying a large cooking pot, and perhaps blowing three kisses.
BIG BEAR	*Big Bear Goes Fishing* *Big Bear to the Rescue* (Margolis)	Bear headgear; fishing pole, pail, and tagboard fish. Coil of rope for the second title. Could add Squirrel, Spotted Pony, Owl and the other characters from *Big Bear to the Rescue*.
BLACKBOARD BEAR	*Blackboard Bear* *And My Mean Old Mother Will Be Sorry, Blackboard Bear* *I Sure Am Glad to See You, Blackboard Bear* *We're in Big Trouble, Blackboard Bear* (Alexander)	Could be represented simply by Anthony, chalk in hand, carrying a small blackboard with a drawing of a bear. Depending on the title selected, the following could be added: cross mother, shaking her finger at Anthony in pajamas with jar of honey in his hand; bully taking away Anthony's ice cream cone; the wished-for playmates—the cowboy and the Indian; or a teddy bear in overalls. Blackboard Bear could be a second child, larger than Anthony, and could be carrying the goldfish, honey, and/or blueberries from the final title.
BORIS	*Morris and Boris* *Halloween with Morris and Boris* *Morris Has a Cold* *Morris Tells Boris Mother Moose Stories and Rhymes* (Wiseman)	Bear headgear. If alone, a sign, "Peter Piper picked a peck of pickled peppers" would communicate the tongue twister incident. Preferably, Boris would be escorting Morris, his antlers in place, and would be perhaps handing him a tissue for his cold. Dialogue taken from the Mother Moose mix-ups would be crowd pleasing. See page 10 for suggestions regarding the Halloween title.
CAT IN THE HAT	*The Cat in the Hat* *The Cat in the Hat Comes Back* (Dr. Seuss)	Essential: Hat as described on pages 24–25. Nice to add: Black clothing; tail; white gloves; white paper or fabric breast front; large red bow for tie. Should have a swaggering gait and give victory gestures. Props might include fish in a bowl or dress with red spot pinned on it. Could be joined by the two children, Sally with an exaggerated bow on her head, both shaking their fingers disapprovingly at the Cat in the Hat. Thing One and Thing Two could also be included.

CHARACTER	AUTHOR AND TITLE(S)	COSTUME, PROP, ACTION, PARTNER IDEAS
CHARLES	*Keep Your Mouth Closed, Dear* (Aliki)	Bag or box headgear needs second structure for crocodile snout. Props might include any or all of the following: can of baby powder; alarm clock; wooden spoon; soap; or other items Charles swallowed. Could be joined by mother crocodile carrying a large chocolate cake, or replica thereof, or hauling a canister vacuum cleaner.
CHALKS	*The Chalk Box Story* (Freeman) 	This would make a good class entry. Seven students may be walking chalks, each wrapped in a different color paper, with a cone-shaped hat of the same color. Or the students may simply carry body-sized chalks. A large picture of the desert island may be carried between two chalks or by a boy and a turtle. The latter would wear a sandwich body as well as turtle headgear.
CHINESE BROTHERS	*The Five Chinese Brothers* (Bishop)	Nylon stocking head cover, ideally long enough to braid into a pigtail; black coolie hat. (Joining the edges of the the V with a slight overlap produces a lovely hat.) Uniform white paper tops could be made but windbreakers turned backwards and arms folded to conceal hands would be satisfactory. The five look-alikes would be sufficient to illustrate this book. Special effects might be used if only one or two are represented. First Chinese brother would be puffing his cheeks out, having swallowed the sea, and would be gesturing frantically to a little boy with seashells in his arms to come back. A talented stilt walker who covered his stilts with very long adult pants volunteered to be the second Chinese brother at my school one year. 

Note: Suggestion has been made that this story has unfair racial stereotyping. I tend to think of it as a very beloved folk tale, however, and still enjoy it with children. You may want to read it thoughtfully before accepting or rejecting it.

Characters from Picture Story Books

CHARACTER	AUTHOR AND TITLE(S)	COSTUME, PROP, ACTION, PARTNER IDEAS
CLAUDE	*Claude the Dog, a Christmas Story* *Claude and Pepper* (Gackenbach)	Dog headgear; three boxes in Christmas wrappings; or the pillow, plaid blanket, and mouse that he received as gifts. Could be accompanied by Bummer (a small dog) or by a young boy giving Claude hugs and receiving licks from him. (A long tongue would help in the latter.)
CLIFFORD	*Clifford the Big Red Dog* and many other titles, all beginning with *Clifford* or *Clifford's* (Bridwell)	Headgear as on page 21. Could wear black cape and carry devil's spear for *Clifford's Halloween*.
CORDUROY	*Corduroy* *A Pocket for Corduroy* (Freeman)	Bear headgear. Corduroy overalls are most desirable, one button missing and strap flopping. Could be joined by Lisa simulating sewing on a button. Or Lisa could carry an overall-clad Teddy bear and be sewing either a button or a pocket on.
CURIOUS GEORGE	Several titles, all beginning *Curious George . . .* (H. A. Rey)	A nylon cap works well in lieu of box headgear. Brown clothing is nice. Props again depend on the title or incident selected.
	Curious George Gets a Medal	"Astronaut" coveralls and a large yellow construction paper medal hung around George's neck.
	Curious George Rides a Bike	Bicycle; paperboy's delivery bag; newspapers folded into boats.
	Curious George Takes a Job	Cloth in hand; pail hung from belt; window washing tool; blue cap.

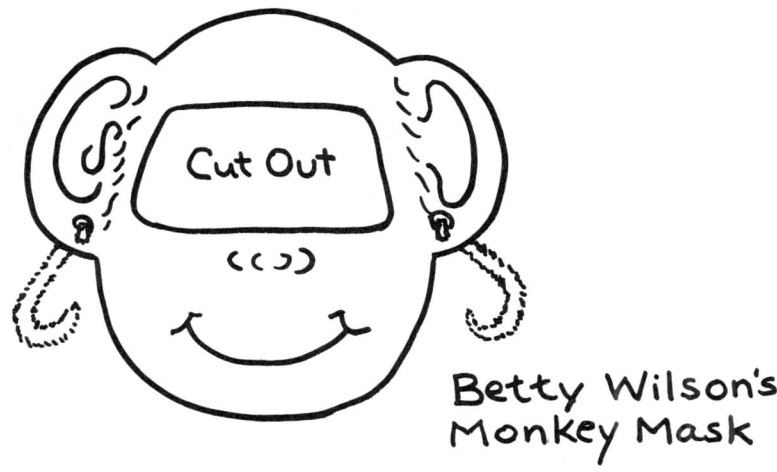

Betty Wilson's Monkey Mask

CHARACTER	AUTHOR AND TITLE(S)	COSTUME, PROP, ACTION, PARTNER IDEAS
	Curious George Goes to the Hospital	Jigsaw puzzle with George pretending to eat a piece. This title will work well for a float representation: Curious George on a wagon hospital bed, solicitously attended by a nurse and doctor with appropriate medical clothing and gear. George could be joined also by the man in the big yellow hat. (Use the design for a top hat but extend the brim much further.)
CUT-UPS	*The Cut-Ups* (James Marshall)	Spud Jenkins and Joe Turner could simply replicate the masks on the first page. Or, they could, with sign, makers, and megaphone in hand, copy Spud's "Tattoo Parlor." More exciting would be to add a moustached, aviator-capped Mr. Spurgle who would chase them, if not in his wheelchair, then hobbling on cast and cane, pausing to threaten them while brandishing the cane. A red-haired Mary Frances, in her green glasses, would amplify the scene. She could drive a homemade sports car or just have her arms full of toys. Of course, she would be laughing.
DANNY	*Danny and the Dinosaur* (Hoff)	School clothing. Must be accompanied by a dinosaur. A box headgear base worn by one person would support the long neck and head for the diplodoccus but perhaps the dinosaur would be more effective with a two-person body . . . allowing a lightweight Danny to ride on it. An upright dinosaur and Danny might have ice cream cones as props. A hide and seek game with the other children might be enacted.
DIGGINGEST DOG	*The Diggingest Dog* (Perkins)	Dog headgear; cardboard model of Mrs. Thwaites' fence, so labelled; uprooted flowers with their clumps of soil in child's "paws."
DOCTOR DE SOTO	*Doctor De Soto* (Steig)	Mouse headgear with glasses drawn in; large jar labelled "glue"; narrow paint brush. Could be joined by the fox with bandage around his head and jaw, gesturing pain from tooth, and/or by his wife who might carry a large "gold" tooth.
FERDINAND	*The Story of Ferdinand* (Leaf)	Box headgear with horns. Could be a two-person bull with a blanket cover. Should be smelling a bunch of flowers, held by an upright self, or in the case of a two-person

Characters from Picture Story Books

CHARACTER	AUTHOR AND TITLE(S)	COSTUME, PROP, ACTION, PARTNER IDEAS
		creation, by a pretty lady. Could be accompanied by a matador (hat, cape, and sword) or bee (wings and striped body on sandwich board.)
FOX	*One Fine Day* (Hogrogian)	Fox headgear; red clothing. Could be carrying a milk can so labelled and should be holding his rear end with cries of pain. Should be accompanied by an old woman, in long skirt and babushka holding a knife in one hand and the fox's tail in the other, showing anger. Could also be joined by the cow, field (sandwich board), stream, maiden, pedlar, hen, and miller with their props. A good selection for a class production.
FRANCES	*A Baby Sister for Frances* *A Bargain for Frances* *Bedtime for Frances* *Best Friends for Frances* *A Birthday for Frances* *Bread and Jam for Frances* (Russell Hoban)	Badger headgear. Props would vary with the title. A plastic tea set would represent Frances in *A Bargain for Frances*, bread and jam or a plateful of runny eggs, *Bread and Jam for Frances*. Gloria could accompany Frances for the *Best Friends* title and they could pull a wagon, loaded with picnic hamper, jar with two frogs, balloons, lollipops, etc. They would carry a sign, "BEST FRIENDS OUTING - NO BOYS." If Albert accompanied them, the "NO BOYS" would be crossed out, Albert would be carrying a snake in a pillow case, and the three would be holding balloons.
FROG	*Jump, Frog, Jump* (Kalan)	Excellent bag frog head illustrated in Chernoff's costume book. The frog would be jumping. A large black fly could be suspended in front of the frog's mouth by a thread. May be chased by three boys, trying to put a basket over his head. Other characters, the fish, snake, and turtle, may be added and one of the boys might carry a net. This title would also make a good project for a class. A pond backdrop could be painted as well.
FROG	*Days with Frog and Toad*	Frog headgear (see Chernoff) for both characters. Toad's costume should be made of brown for a somewhat smaller child. For "The Kite" Toad could be waving a kite above his head, jumping up and down, and shouting, "UP KITE UP." Frog would follow, holding the ball of string.

Representing Children's Book Characters

CHARACTER	AUTHOR AND TITLE(S)	COSTUME, PROP, ACTION, PARTNER IDEAS
	Frog and Toad Are Friends	Or, Frog, wearing Toad's gift of the jacket covered with buttons, could rest his arm companionably over the shoulders of jacketless Toad, in representation of the chapter, "The Button."
	Frog and Toad Together	Or, both, dressed as they normally appear, could be gobbling cookies from a bowl as they did in "Cookies."
	Also Frog and Toad All Year (Lobel)	
FROG	*The Princess and Froggie* (Zemach)	Frog headgear (see Chernoff). Froggie would be holding a green lollipop (oversize, please) and could be comforting a crying princess (dress with sash in bow.) Or, Princess could be throwing a blue ball while holding a red lollipop. May also be accompanied by a king, in robes and crown, wearing an artificial bird on top of the crown. The king would be expressing anger at the presence of the bird.
FROSTY	*Frosty the Snowman* (Bedford)	Snowman costume as in Chernoff's costume book. See p. 29. Would be carrying a broom and dancing to his music. (A portable tape recorder would do the trick.)
FUNNY LITTLE WOMAN	*The Funny Little Woman* (Mosel)	Kimona; paddle; rice ball. Accompanying children with Jizo Sama stick puppets and/or green bag headgear for the wicked *oni*. The latter could be chasing the funny little woman.
GEORGE	*George and Martha*	Box headgear with smaller box or bag snout. George could be roller skating. Should have one white tooth and one gold tooth. A less dangerous portrayal would include Martha with a pot labelled "split pea soup" offering George a plate of chocolate chip cookies. George might hold a loafer shoe filled with green material.
	George and Martha Encore	George, wearing a serape and a Mexican hat, could be performing a hat dance. Martha in wings and skirt would be dancing the happy butterfly dance.
	George and Martha One Fine Day	
	George and Martha Rise and Shine	George might be running away from Martha and her snake, crying, "Eeek!"
	George and Martha Tons of Fun (Marshall)	

Characters from Picture Story Books

CHARACTER	AUTHOR AND TITLE(S)	COSTUME, PROP, ACTION, PARTNER IDEAS
GEORGIE	Many titles all beginning *Georgie* or *Georgie's . . .* (Bright)	See pages 6 and 9.
(MY) GRANDFATHER	*The Mitten* (Tresselt)	Boy wearing winter clothing could carry a huge red paper mitten, bulging with stuffed animals. (This book is ideal for a class presentation, a child representing each animal, with remaining children utilized as trees for the forest.)
GROUCHY LADYBUG	*The Grouchy Ladybug* (Carle)	Sandwich board circles; headband-anchored antennae. Child should be glowering and be yelling, "Hey, you! Want to fight?" Any number of the appropriate adversaries, the yellow jacket, the gorilla, etc., could be added.
GUS	*Gus Was a Friendly Ghost* *Gus Was a Gorgeous Ghost* (Thayer)	See pages 7 and 10.
HAPPY LION	Several titles, all beginning *The Happy Lion . . .* (Fatio)	Lion headgear. Accompanied by lionness with green eyes. Francois, in beret, shorts, and knee sox would be between them.
HAROLD	*Harold and the Purple Crayon* *Harold's Trip to the Sky* *A Picture for Harold's Room* (Johnson)	Student would wear purple clothing, including Harold's characteristic cap. The crayon could be represented by a person or a model, but do include the trademark for Crayola. Harold could carry a large drawing of a star (in purple) or a cardboard model of a rocket.
HARRY	*Harry the Dirty Dog* *Harry and the Lady Next Door* *Harry and the Sea* *No Roses for Harry* (Zion)	Dog headgear; white clothing with black spots pinned on. Scrubbing brush for the first title. A girl in a long dress holding sheet music and singing could represent the lady next door. Harry would be covering his ears in this case. For the title *No Roses for Harry*, a "nest" constructed out of a flowery wool garment could hold a "bird" and in turn, be held by Harry.
HORTON	*Horton Hatches an Egg*	Elephant headgear; nest; large cardboard or styrofoam egg. Could include a Maizie-bird waving goodbye or hovering around the nest. Horton could be repeating his "I meant what I said, I said what . . " continuously.

CHARACTER	AUTHOR AND TITLE(S)	COSTUME, PROP, ACTION, PARTNER IDEAS
	Horton Hears a Who (Seuss)	Horton would hold clover, listening carefully for the Whos. Or, the Whos could be life-size (with headcovers from nylons to which tufts are attached) and make noise with various kettles, cans, garbage can lids, bazookas, etc. A JoJo should be included to say "Yopp!"
HOUND	*Hound and Bear*	Dog and bear headgear. Hound might have a bucket labelled "black paint" and a ladder; Bear would be in his nightgown, acting out anger. Another incident could be represented by Hound and Bear carrying several opened gift boxes along with the wrappings and ribbon while admiring Bear's new hat.
	More from Hound and Bear (Gackenbach)	Hound might wear sunglasses and be walking on stilts.
HUMBUG WITCH	*Humbug Witch* (Balian)	See page 11.
IRA	*Ira Sleeps Over* (Waber)	Ira and Reggie in pajamas, carrying Teddy bears labelled, "Tah Tah" and "Foo Foo." They could stop in front of the audience to have a pillow fight. Or Ira could proceed first, accompanied by his sister, shaking her finger at him and saying, threateningly, "He'll laugh!"
JOHNNY LION	*Johnny Lion's Bad Day*	Lion headgear; nightwear; medicine bottle with red medicine. Could be showing fright at an owl accompanying him.
	Johnny Lion's Boots (Hurd)	Rubber boots; box to hide in while Mother and Father Lion look for him.
KAPIT	*Bringing the Rain to Kapiti Plain* (Aardema)	Fabric or paper tunic, draped off one shoulder; arm bracelets; staff. Should stand on one leg "like big stork bird." Could have bow and large feather arrow and shoot at a dark cloud (worn by another student.) Could be joined by brown grass, cows, an eagle shedding a feather, lightning, rain, and green grass in a class production.
KATY	*Katy No-Pocket* (Payne)	Kangaroo headgear; brown clothing; wide tail; carpenter's apron, with pockets filled with stuffed animals. Should travel by hopping.

Characters from Picture Story Books

CHARACTER	AUTHOR AND TITLE(S)	COSTUME, PROP, ACTION, PARTNER IDEAS
KNIGHT	*The Knight and the Dragon* (De Paola)	Foil-wrapped box "helmet"; shield; lance or sword for knight's costume. Dragon headgear. The pair could be rushing at each other and missing contact each time, or a representation of the final K & D Bar-B-Q could be made with the addition of a sign, a chef's hat and a grill for the dragon, and an apron for the knight.
LAZY TOMMY	*Lazy Tommy Pumpkinhead* (Du Bois)	Representation might work best by having Tommy seated on a wagon, as on the second last page of the story, surrounded by the mess of food or labelled replicas thereof. A budding engineer might enjoy the challenge of creating a toothbrushing machine (boxes on a second child would do) and, naturally, Tommy's toes would be brushed.
LENTIL	*Lentil* (McCloskey)	Boy in school clothing twirling a jackknife on a chain around his finger and playing a harmonica. Could be joined by Old Sneep in hobo-type clothing, sucking noisily on a lemon. Band players and Colonel Carter himself could also be included.
LITTLE BEAR	*Little Bear's Thanksgiving*	Bear headgear. Could appear alone merely carrying a pumpkin pie. Or, could be asleep on a wagon/bed float, surrounded by Squirrel, Owl, Sparrow, and Squeaky, waking only when they call out, "Pumpkin pie!"
	Little Bear Marches in the St. Patrick's Day Parade Other titles, all beginning *Little Bear's . . .* (Janice)	Little Bear would wear a green hat and carry an opened umbrella. A stuffed mouse for Squeaky could be attached to his shoulder. The addition of any number of children with signs, shamrock emblems, and green clothing for the parade would make a good class production.
LITTLE BEAR	*A Kiss for Little Bear* Other titles include *Little Bear, Father Bear Comes Home, Little Bear's Friend,* and *Little Bear's Visit* (Minarik)	Bear headgear; artist's paintbrush; duplicate of his monster picture that was sent to his grandmother. The other animals, including the kissing skunks, and grandmother could be added.
LITTLE GIRL	*The Gunniwolf* (Harper)	Dress; bouquet with pink, white, and orange flowers. Student may sing, "Kum qua qui wa, kum qua ki wa." An accompanying gunniwolf would be best in a hooded jump

CHARACTER	AUTHOR AND TITLE(S)	COSTUME, PROP, ACTION, PARTNER IDEAS
		suit with his or her own face visible, so that he can feign sleep and then open one eye, see little girl running away, and chase her.
LITTLE OLD LADY	*The Little Old Lady Who Was Not Afraid of Anything* (Linda Williams)	The little old lady (bun, hat, dress, apron, basket) needs to have at least some of the following to which to say, "Get out of my way, I'm not afraid of you:-" the clopping shoes; the wiggling pants; the shaking shirt; the clapping gloves; the nodding hat; and the booing "pumpkin head." Large adult-sized items manipulated by children would work for the first three articles; oversize handicrafted items would be best for the latter three. A class could easily chorus the repeated cumulative narration.
LITTLE RABBIT	*The Little Rabbit Who Wanted Red Wings* (Bailey)	See page 12.
LITTLE RABBIT	*Little Rabbit's Loose Tooth* (Bate)	See pages 7 and 13.
MADAME BODOT	*Crictor* (Ungerer)	Long dress; high heels; hair in bun; pince-nez, real or pipe cleaner variety. Could be cradling a stuffed snake and pretending to feed him milk from a baby bottle, or could be showing the crowd a fancy medal resting around Crictor's neck. The burglar and the gendarme could be added.
MAX	*Where the Wild Things Are* (Sendak)	Jump suit with tail; hood or cap made from nylons with ears attached; crown; sceptre. May brandish fork or use the "Be still" gesture, arms up, staring without blinking. One or more monsters under his control or doing wild rumpus activities would enhance the representation.
MISS VIOLA SWAMP	*Miss Nelson Is Missing* (Allard)	Black clothing; Halloween witch wig; mean face; school pointer. Would need to be accompanied by at least one small student to whom she would say, "Straighten up now." A small group of students, each loaded with many textbooks, would be walking sedately under her control. This group might be preceded by a blond-haired, sweetly smiling Miss Nelson with her class following her, talking noisily, jostling one another, throwing spitballs, etc.

Characters from Picture Story Books

CHARACTER	AUTHOR AND TITLE(S)	COSTUME, PROP, ACTION, PARTNER IDEAS
MR. GUMPY	*Mr. Gumpy's Outing* (Burningham)	Shirt; trousers; straw hat; pole. A backdrop of a boat on the river may be used or a second child could wear the boat as a sandwich board. May be joined by a kicking goat, a trampling calf, flapping chickens, a bleating sheep, a pig mucking about, a dog teasing a cat who, in turn, is chasing a hopping rabbit, and a pair of squabbling children.
	Also, *Mr. Gumpy's Motor Car*	
MR. PENNY	*The Ghost with the Halloween Hiccups* (Mooser)	See page 10.
MR. WILLOWBY	*Mr. Willowby's Christmas Tree* (Barry)	Bald head; suit. Could be accompanied by Baxter the butler with a saw in his hand, or preferably, or in addition, a tree top on a silver platter. They could be joined by all the other characters, each subsequent recipient of the tree top holding a smaller version of the tree. Mr. Willowby's large tree could be represented by a person.
NAMELESS CHARACTERS	*Cloudy with a Chance of Meatballs* (Barrett)	This would be a group effort, preceded by a signbearer with the town's name, "Chew and Swallow." One student could represent the weather forecaster, pointing to a large chart showing clouds and meatballs. Another might carry a plate of cheese, a clothespin clipped on his nose. Two students could stagger under the weight of a giant donut or hamburger carried between them. Other students might wear raincoats and boots and carry upturned umbrellas. They could point at the sky and pantomime catching a shower of orange juice, for example. Still others could be draped with tendrils of spaghetti (yarn) and hold a replica of the newspaper headline, "Spaghetti Ties Up Town."
NATE THE GREAT	*Nate the Great** and several other titles all beginning, *Nate the Great and . . .* (Marjorie Sharmat)	Nate, wearing his belted trench coat, Sherlock Holmes hat, and rubbers could be forking in his trademark pancakes. Or, for the initial title, he could be in regular school clothes and be sporting red paint on his face and clothing (make-up and paper). Harry and Annie, each with a paintbrush (red and yellow respectively) should join him and carry oversize copies of Harry's

CHARACTER	AUTHOR AND TITLE(S)	COSTUME, PROP, ACTION, PARTNER IDEAS
		pictures, including one of the orange "monster with three heads." Fang himself could also be portrayed.
OLD BLACK WITCH	*Old Black Witch* (Devlin)	See page 11.
OLD LADY	*I Know an Old Lady Who Swallowed a Fly* (Bonne)	Black-clothed student with very protruding stomach. Could be carried on a stretcher. Could be joined by the fly, spider, cat, dog, goat, and horse.
ORSON	*The Easter Egg Artists* (Adams)	See page 12.
PEDLAR	*Caps for Sale* (Slobodkina)	Suit; gray, brown, blue, and red caps for head on top of checked cap, if alone. For a minimum representation the pedlar needs to have his one checked cap and be shaking his finger at one monkey, a cap in hand, the monkey, in turn, shaking his finger back at the pedlar. The addition of any number of monkeys plus the subsequent action would heighten the effect.
PETER	*Peter's Chair**	Boy carrying chair.
	*Whistle for Willie**	Boy partially hidden under cardboard box, followed by student in dachshund headgear. Or, student, carrying toy dachshund, trying to whistle, drawing on the sidewalk with chalk, and making turns with arms outstretched. Or, student could wear a large fedora and be looking in a hand mirror.
	*A Snowy Day** (Keats)	Student, dressed in winter clothing, dragging sled, and putting a styrofoam snowball in his pocket. Could stop to do snow angel motions on the grass.
PETER RABBIT	*The Tale of Peter Rabbit* (Potter)	See page 13.
PIGGY	*Piggy in the Puddle* (Pomerantz)	Pig headgear; bonnet; yellow dress; balloon or umbrella; sign, saying "Nope—No Soap."
RUNAWAY BUNNY	*The Runaway Bunny* (Margaret Wise Brown)	See page 13.
SAM	*Popcorn* (Asch)	Bear headgear; Indian headband with feather on top of bear head; loin cloth. Could be

Characters from Picture Story Books

CHARACTER	AUTHOR AND TITLE(S)	COSTUME, PROP, ACTION, PARTNER IDEAS
		carrying a large bag of popcorn and a broom. Could be accompanied by his mother, dressed as a rabbit, and father, in clown costume, offering him more popcorn. The other characters could be added: Betty, a witch, with Black cat popcorn; king Billy, carrying his Royal popcorn on a pillow; the ballerina with Tiptoe popcorn; the devil with Red hot popcorn, etc.
SAM	*Sam** (Scott)	School clothing; rolling pin; tart tin with pastry shells. Or, student could be carrying a chair into which he puts his head. Could be crying and comforted by his mother who carries the rolling pin and tart tin.
SKELETONS	*Funnybones* (Ahlberg)	Tall student and shorter student, wearing dark clothing or black plastic garbage bags, with white construction paper bones taped on in the form of a skeleton. Both would wear a skull face mask and the tall one would wear a red top hat with a blue band. They would simulate scaring one another. One might carry a garbage can, climb in, and pop out with a big "Boo!" as the other approached. A stuffed dog might be carried or a student, willing to walk on hands and knees might play the dog and chase thrown sticks.
SNEETCH	*The Sneetches and Other Stories* (Dr. Seuss)	Jump suit with yellow paper or tagboard star fastened on belly. A stocking mask would include strings of construction paper tufts on top of the head and the circlet around the neck could be made from feathers or shredded paper. Could carry stick threaded with a weiner or marshmallows or could be paying $10 (large replica) to McBean (green hat and bow tie) who might carry a sign, "$10 to be the best Sneetches."
STUPIDS	*The Stupids Step Out* *The Stupids Have a Ball* *The Stupids Die* (Allard)	See page 12 and page 112.
TAILOR	*The Bed Just So* (Hardendorff)	Trousers; white shirt; vest. Could carry ironing board and iron and fall asleep on top of the board. Could wear a nightgown

CHARACTER	AUTHOR AND TITLE(S)	COSTUME, PROP, ACTION, PARTNER IDEAS
		and nightcap, clutch a sheet and express fear. A pot or wicker laundry basket with a doll pillow and cover inside, or a hammock could be carried in lieu of the sheet. The "wise woman" in purple might accompany him.
UNCLE UBB	*Dr. Seuss' ABC* (Dr. Seuss)	Long white underwear; moustache; opened umbrella; large *U* on chest.
VERY HUNGRY CATERPILLAR	*The Very Hungry Caterpillar* (Carle)	Headgear with antennae, see page 18. Should hold tummy as if ill. May be accompanied by a large cardboard apple or the items eaten on the day of overindulgence: watermelon, cupcake, pickle, etc. (A round hole should appear in each item.) The "beautiful butterfly" may be presented also.
WILBUR	*The Bionic Bunny Show* (Laurene Krasny Brown & Marc Brown)	See page 13.
WILD BABY (Ben)	*The Wild Baby* Also, *The Wild Baby Goes to Sea* (Lindgren)	May be simply costumed as a blue sack. Or could wear his green coveralls and be attacking his hair (artificial locks on a nylon cap) with scissors to the remonstrances of mama. Might also be licking a second child in wolf headgear.

WIZARD	*The Case of the Hungry Stranger** (Bonsall)	Casual clothes. Wizard would lead Tubby (fat and eating, perhaps tangled in a garden hose); Skinny (thin); and Snitch (smaller); and carry the sign from the clubhouse,
		   "NO GIRLS
		   THE WIZARD
		   PRIVATE EYE"
		The coterie could be joined by Mrs. Meech (dress, apron, blue teeth, and blueberry pie) and the following, each with big blue smiles: the mailman; the ice cream salesman; the paper boy; and the dog, Mop. Mop's owner, Marigold (glasses and dress), could finally join the four boys in eating blueberry pie.

---

*These titles include black children, who may be portrayed by non-black students. The titles may be especially desirable, however, in matching a black child with a character with whom he might be proud to identify, knowing also that he would be the best choice for the representation.

VII. IDEAS FOR CHARACTERS FROM FICTION

FICTION, OTHER THAN THE PICTURE story book variety, takes some commitment of time for reading. Such time for recreational reading, available in years past, has a tendency to be utilized now for television viewing, and video and computer use. As a result, there may be less wide recognition of specific fiction titles now than in the past. Certainly, there is less acquaintance with titles and characters from longer fiction than those from picture books.

Those books made into movies, of course, are well known, and the perenially favorite Cleary and Blume titles are similar exceptions to the general statement above. The adventures in which the reader, as central character, makes multiple choices as to the direction of the plot also enjoy current popularity; however, such adventures do not yield memorable characters that one would want to represent in a book celebration.

Nonetheless, when classroom teachers are committed to reading aloud on a daily basis, when principals are committed to encouraging school-wide silent reading periods, and when librarians are committed to promotion of the reading of fiction, the picture becomes brighter from the point of view of the bibliophile. And, hopefully, the book parade will stimulate additional interest in the reading of fiction.

Probably the most productive source for ideas for costumed book characters is the fantasy genre, which includes those titles claimed by the world of film, most notably *Charlie and the Chocolate Factory*, *Pippi Longstocking*, *Mary Poppins*, and *The Wizard of Oz*. The characters from fantasy most often are unique and their qualities are easily portrayed.

With a little thought, however, the characters from realistic fiction may also be represented. Of course, the idiosyncrasies that make them special would be shown for them as for characters from fantasy. In addition, however, and with the longer texts associated with the fiction category of books, one most often would need to focus on a single episode within a title to show circumstances unique to that character rather than the universal qualities of the character. With realistic fiction, then, it is even more important to isolate a very particular incident from the book and to concentrate on this incident in planning for the props. Frequently, too, more dialogue may have to be used to reveal the characters.

For example, Henry Huggins could be depicted with his cardboard box and Ribsy, as suggested on page 7, and as taken from the chapter entitled, "Henry and Ribs." One *could* choose, however, to work on the chapter, "Henry's Green Christmas," and make large green ears for Henry, in addition to placing green spots and smudges on his face, shoulders, and clothing. You might have Henry escorted by Scooter, carrying a pail of green paint and a paintbrush or exclaimed over by his teacher, "Oh, Henry! I knew I shouldn't have allowed them to use real paint!" A barking Ribsy, running around the group would complete the scene nicely.

Fiction titles presented on parade at Erie School have included the following:

CHARACTER	AUTHOR AND TITLE(S)	COSTUME, PROP, ACTION, PARTNER, AND DIALOGUE IDEAS
ABEL	*Abel's Island* (Steig)	Mouse headgear; frayed trousers; stained, tattered shirt. Might be sniffing and caressing Amanda's gauze scarf or dragging along his "boat," a large spike in a board, panting

CHARACTER	AUTHOR AND TITLE(S)	COSTUME, PROP, ACTION, PARTNER, AND DIALOGUE IDEAS
		as he would in his struggle in the river. Might be accompanied by Frog, Gower Glackens, pretending to swim away from Abel and waving goodbye, with a "I'll be sure to send help."
ALICE	*Alice's Adventures in Wonderland* (Carroll)	Full skirted dress, preferably a solid color; "Mary Jane" shoes; long hair; bow; bottle with label, "DRINK ME." Might be nibbling on a piece of cake, labelled, "EAT ME," and wondering out loud what might result from eating it. Partner might be the White Rabbit (pink nose, please), drawing a large pocket watch from his waistcoat and saying worriedly, "Oh, dear! Oh, dear! I shall be too late!"
ANDREW	*Freckle Juice* (Blume)	A spectacled second grade boy, holding a large replica of "Sharon's Secret Recipe for Freckle Juice" list, would be covered with blue marker dots. Sharon, holding a large 50¢ piece (oversize), could be running her tongue over her teeth, or, more dramatically, be making a frog face. Nicky with his hundreds of freckles could be included. (The scene where Andrew pushes the money, wrapped in a tissue, over to Sharon's desk, followed by Sharon throwing a folded paper—the recipe—back, and Andrew's subsequent fall to the floor arousing the attention of Miss Kelly would make an amusing dramatization.)

APE FACE (Ben)	*Summer Switch* Other titles: *Freaky Friday* and *A Billion for Boris* (Rogers)	Taller boy in man's suit and beard would be holding a pink plush hippo pajama bag cradled in his arms and standing with his shoe against his leg like a stork. He would be accompanied by a small frowning boy (*really* Ben's father, Bill Andrews) wearing a T-shirt on which would be printed
		    SOONA
		    WISSA
		    KIT
		The small boy would be pulling on a third character's hand (the mother, Ellen Andrews) in a tantrum. "I don't wanna, I don't wanna. I'm not gonna. Puleeze don't make me."

ASLAN	*The Lion, the Witch, and the Wardrobe* (Lewis)	Lion headgear with emphasis on the "great solemn overwhelming eyes" on an oversized mask attached to a box. Aslan, his four

Characters from Fiction

CHARACTER	AUTHOR AND TITLE(S)	COSTUME, PROP, ACTION, PARTNER, AND DIALOGUE IDEAS
		paws tied together, could be borne across the stage by hags and ogres. He could be joined by the four children in adult-sized winter coats and/or by the White Witch. The latter would wear white make-up (talcum on a vaseline base) and bright red lipstick and would carry her golden wand.
BEEZUS	*Beezus and Ramona* (Cleary)	School clothing for nine-year-old. Perhaps the "party" to which Ramona, age 4, had invited many preschoolers, unbeknownst to her mother, could be focused on. Beezus would be organizing the parade with a drum, a horn, and yardsticks and rulers with handkerchiefs for flags for the young children and an eggbeater for baby, Willa Jean. They all would march, saying, "Bingle-bongle-by."
BENJY	*Benjy in Business* Other titles: *Benjy and the Power of the Zingies; Benjy the Football Hero* (Van Leeuwen)	A boy in summer clothing typical of an eight-year-old could merely be caressing and showing off a new baseball mitt. The mitt should have a visible "signature" (of Clyde Johnson) on it and a tag labelled $22.95 dangling from it. An alternative idea would be to have Benjy carry a monkey bank and show his calculations on a large tagboard "paper." $22.95—mitt $2.52—so far $20.43 to go In this case, a sad, discouraged look on his face would be appropriate. Or, Benjy, carrying on a stick the cardboard sign that advertised "Odd Jobs Man" and listed all the services available could be joined by his friend Jason. Jason would pull a wagon loaded with the rake, broom, bucket, watering can, etc.
BILLY FORRESTER	*How to Eat Fried Worms* (Rockwell)	Casual clothing. Could be accompanied by Alan, Joe, and Tom. The scene in which the first worm was eaten could be played. The orange crate, loaded with ketchup, Worcestershire, mustard, salt, pepper, horseradish, etc. would be carried on stage. The worm would be resting on a silver platter and would be served and uncovered with a flourish by Alan, "Vurm a la mud!" Billy would recoil, "Awrgh!" Joe would

CHARACTER	AUTHOR AND TITLE(S)	COSTUME, PROP, ACTION, PARTNER, AND DIALOGUE IDEAS
		have a napkin over his arm like a wine steward, and Tom would say, "Allow me," and proceed to ketchup and mustard the worm and use the knife and fork to feed Billy. (The worm could be one constructed out of something less offensive than the real thing!)
BLUBBER (Linda)	*Blubber* (Blume)	Girl would wear pillows for plumpness. She might show a drawing of blubber and say, "My report is uh . . . on the whale. Blubber is a thick layer of fat that lies under the skin and over the muscles of whales." Could be joined by Robby, his whole body shaking with laughter, by Wendy, hiccupping, and by other classmates, laughing. If your stomach is strong, Bruce could join in, also, picking his nose.
BLUE-NOSED. WITCH	*The Blue-Nosed Witch* (Embry)	See page 12.
BUNNICULA	*Bunnicula* *The Celery Stalks at Midnight* (Howe)	Rabbit headgear, pointed fangs visible; white clothing; black cape. Could carry oversized models of vegetables, all white, labelled, "tomato," "lettuce," etc. Could be accompanied by Harold (dog head) and Chester (cat), at a distance, whispering as though talking about Bunnicula.
CASEY VALENTINE	*Fourth Grade Celebrity* *Left-Handed Shortstop* (Giff)	School clothes. Could be reading aloud from an oversized copy of the *Ogden School Observer*, clearly printed with the headline, "Casey Valentine Receives Medals for Saving the Ogden School from Tremendous Fire." Might be accompanied by a spectacled Walter, wearing a cast on his left arm. (But this representation would indicate the second title.)
CASSIE STEPHENS	*The Pistachio Prescription* (Danziger)	Typical high school girl outfit; bag, labelled, "pistachio nuts"; dark glasses; eyebrows covered by a narrow strip of flesh-colored tissue (stuck on with sugar water). Could be met by friend, Vicki. "Hi! Why are you wearing those sunglasses? It's going to rain today!" Cassie's reply would be, "Promise not to laugh?" After receiving assurance that Vicki would not laugh, Cassie would remove the sunglasses and Vicki would collapse into a screaming giggle. Cassie would walk off, eating nuts.

Characters from Fiction

CHARACTER	AUTHOR AND TITLE(S)	COSTUME, PROP, ACTION, PARTNER, AND DIALOGUE IDEAS
CHARLIE	*Charlie and the Chocolate Factory* (Dahl)	Shabby, ragged clothing, including cap; oversize chocolate bar, labelled, "Wonka's Whipple-Scrumptious Fudge-mallow Delight." Charlie could open the wrapper of the chocolate bar and pull out the Golden Ticket, jumping up and down with delight. Could be accompanied by many additional characters. See page 116 for suggestions.
CHARLOTTE	*Charlotte's Web* (White)	See page 16 for two different methods of costuming. See page 15 for suggestions for scene and/or additional characters.
CHESTER	*The Cricket in Times Square* Other titles: *Harry Cat's Pet Puppy; Tucker's Countryside* (Selden)	Cricket headgear. Body as paper sandwich board. Could be showing distress at munched in half $2 bill (a large drawn and labelled one). "Oh dear, oh dear!" Tucker Mouse and Harry Cat might enter with large coins (foil constructed) in their mouths. It would be nice to add a music background of "Come Back to Sorrento," or "Aida." A different choice of scene might have Mario and the Bellinis selling newspapers and magazines to a number of people who stop to listen to Chester play.
CYBIL ACKERMAN	*The Cybil War* (Byars)	Jeans; tennies; big shirt. Curly red hair would be nice. Should grin and cross her eyes at the audience. The chapter with the pet show could be focused on, and the presentation might include: Cybil's cat, Paw Paw, in grass skirt and lei; Tony's poodle, Miss Vicki, in baby bonnet and diaper (hole for tail); Simon's dog, T-bone, with eyepatch and pirate's hat. The pets could be cardboard models, stuffed animals, children dressed as animals, or, for the brave, the real thing.
DOROTHY	*The Wizard of Oz* (Baum)	Dorothy in full-skirted dress, holding Toto in basket. The rest of the cast may be included: the Lion, Scarecrow, Tin Woodman (foil over tubes of tagboard works well), and the Wizard himself.
DORRIE	Various titles, all beginning *Dorrie* . . .	See page 11.
EEYORE	*Winnie-the-Pooh* (Milne)	Donkey headgear. Could be holding a broken red balloon and an empty honey pot. Christopher Robin could be included, entering with a birthday cake with three

CHARACTER	AUTHOR AND TITLE(S)	COSTUME, PROP, ACTION, PARTNER, AND DIALOGUE IDEAS
		candles and Eeyore's name on it. Winnie and Piglet might join the party. They could hold the balloon and honey pot if Eeyore is costumed as a four-footed animal and this treatment might be the preferred one.
ELLEN TEBBITS	*Ellen Tebbits* (Cleary)	Third grade girl would wear a ballet tutu with a big lump around the waist (representing Ellen's woolen underwear). She would perform abbreviated jumps, frequently stopping to hitch up the lump around her waist. Or, she could be shown in fifth position, imitated by Otis, wearing a jacket, holster, and spurs, and blowing bubble gum. A sign, "Spofford School of Dance," should be visible. Another choice of scene might be the one where Ellen and plump Austine are clapping dusty erasers together, a scene that is important in the book but not as dramatic as others.
ELMER	*My Father's Dragon* Other titles: *Elmer and the Dragon; The Dragons of Blueland* (Gannett)	Boots; short pants; striped shirt; cap; knapsack; tangerine in hand. May be accompanied by a striped dragon with the remains of a rope around his neck, or by any of the animals from Wild Island, with large props in their hands. The Tiger would have chewing gum; the Rhino, a tube of toothpaste; the Gorilla joined by a monkey looking at him with a magnifying glass; and the Crocodile with a lollipop. All but the Dragon might be chasing Elmer.
ELSIE EDWARDS	*Nothing's Fair in Fifth Grade* (DeClements)	Plumpness gained from pillows under a purple housecoat with a ruffled neck. Could focus on the slumber party with Sharon, Diane, and "two cousins" present, in pajamas, all heavily into applying mascara, eyeshadow, and lipstick, looking at themselves in hand mirrors and giggling.
FELINA	*The Little Leftover Witch* (Laughlin)	See page 12.
FERN	*Charlotte's Web* (E. B. White)	Jeans; shirt; baby bottle in hand. Could be pushing a stuffed pig and a doll baby together in a doll carriage.
FRANK THE FLOWER	*The Pushcart War* (Merrill)	Overcoat; tie; vest; trousers; hat with flowers on the brim; pea-pin shooter. Could be holding a sign, "Be Fair to the

Characters from Fiction

CHARACTER	AUTHOR AND TITLE(S)	COSTUME, PROP, ACTION, PARTNER, AND DIALOGUE IDEAS
		Pushcarts" or "18,991 tires!" or could be showing off the accurate placement of some darts on a replica of the crotched pink and green dart board with the 20 trucks pictured. Might be joined by General Anna in her long dress, shawl, and apron, pushing her apple cart, and/or by Maxie Hammerman, the Pushcart King, holding his pin-studded street map of New York City.
FUDGIE (Farley Hatcher)	*Tales of a Fourth Grade Nothing* *Superfudge* (Blume)	Striped T-shirt; blacked-out front two teeth. Could carry empty fish/turtle bowl, be rubbing his tummy, laughing, and saying, "Dribble in tummy." See also pages 9 and 115.
GRANDMAMMA	*The Witches* (Dahl)	Plumpness with pillows; dress; hair in bun; cigar; gold-topped walking stick; black handbag with clasp undone. Should be accompanied by her "darling"—her grandson—in mouse costume, carrying a bottle labelled: Delayed Action Mouse-Maker Formula 86 Could be accompanied by one or more witches, in dresses, pointed toe shoes; wigs, and hats, scratching at their heads. The witches could be scratching scabby bald heads with the addition of nylon head caps.
GREAT AUNT EMMA	*Grinny* (Fisk)	Little old lady dress, opening in the front to reveal electrical wires or perhaps a battery operated light. Could be accompanied by Timmy and Beth sneaking close, peeking at her bodice, expressing shock, and running away.
HENRY	*Henry Huggins* (Cleary)	See page 7 and page 69.
JAMES	*James and the Giant Peach* (Dahl)	Short trousers. Must have large peach, "a rich yellow with patches of pink and red." Include stem, perhaps with strings attached. Could be joined by his whole coterie: Old Green Grasshopper—headgear; sweater; hopping Spider—Include apron and chef's hat. May unroll a ball of string. Ladybug—with 9 spots. Would shake James' hand.

CHARACTER	AUTHOR AND TITLE(S)	COSTUME, PROP, ACTION, PARTNER, AND DIALOGUE IDEAS
		Earthworm—with hat, collar, and tie.
		Centipede—with 42 feet. Boots might be added by someone ambitious at drawing and cutting. Would say, "I'm a pest," or ask someone from the audience to help him off with his boots.
		Silkworm—include fine strand of cord.
		Glow-worm (firefly)—a light or replica thereof could be included on her abdomen.
		The Cloud Men could also be added. See page 10.
JAY BERRY	*Summer of the Monkeys* (Rawls)	Fourteen-year-old in patched trousers and ragged shirt, accompanied by Old Rowdy, his blue tick hound. Could simply carry an apple or a coconut and a book, a large mock one, conspicuously labelled, "Trapping Monkeys in the Jungles of Borneo." Could be joined by Daisy in Red Cross nurse uniform, using crutch. The scene with chimpanzee, Jimbo, offering Jay a tin can of whiskey sour mash, and showing delight when Jay sips it, followed by Jay's subsequent drunk behavior could be played if one had no objections as to its suitability for a school audience. Similarly, showing Jay walking with no "britches" on, holding his aching head would make for much merriment on the part of the viewers if one decided this scene was appropriate for school.
JELLY BELLY (alias Ned or Nat)	*Jelly Belly* (Robert Smith)	Pillows in oversized trousers. Would be stuffing food in mouth. Could be accompanied by Dr. Skinny, wagging his finger disapprovingly while pointing to a scale or a "Camp Lean-Too" sign—and/or—Grandma offering Ned a pitcher of milk and a large cake—and/or—fat friend, Richard, extracting a tennis ball and then corn chips from a tennis ball can.
JULIE (Alias Miyax)	*Julie of the Wolves* (George)	Parka; boots. Could be holding cooking pot and rubbing stomach. Could be joined by the wolf, Kapu. A scene could be played where Julie would close her lips on the bridge of Kapu's nose, grunt-whine, and then bring out a mitten. Kapu would pull the mitten, fall as Julie let go, and then run off with it.

Characters from Fiction

CHARACTER	AUTHOR AND TITLE(S)	COSTUME, PROP, ACTION, PARTNER, AND DIALOGUE IDEAS
LARRY PRYOR	*The Secret Life of the Underwear Champ* (Miles)	Ten-year-old, red head with freckles. Should be obviously made up with lipstick and darkened eyebrows, wear a warm up suit and a helmet that says "Champ," and carry a bat. Could be swinging at a ball pitched by Suzanne in identical warm up suit while a cameraman takes a picture. A big "Champ-Win" sign should be displayed somewhere. If students are brave enough, the same scene would be even better with Larry and Suzanne wearing underwear. The scene could also be expanded with the presence of Arnie, the make-up man adding final touches; Liz, the jeans clad producer, holding a big notebook; the Zigmunds, looking on from their folding chairs; Darlene, the TV mother and catcher; and Frank, the "Dad" and fielder.
LAURA (Ingalls Wilder)	*Little House in the Big Woods* *By the Shores of Plum Creek* *Little House on the Prairie* and several other titles (Laura Ingalls Wilder)	Christmas from *The Little House in the Big Woods* could be focused on with Laura (dark) and Mary (blond) in red flannel nightgowns examining their stockings in which they find bright red mittens and sticks of red and white peppermint candy. Laura would also have a rag doll, Charlotte, "with black button eyes and curly black hair." A little more drama could be extracted from the same title by staging the fight between the two girls while they are collecting chips, chip pans in hand. Mary would say, "Golden hair is better" and Laura would slap Mary. Father would observe the fight and spank Laura with a strap. The subsequent comforting and rocking and the "Well, Laura, my hair is brown." could be added to end on a positive note.
LEIGH BOTTS	*Dear Mr. Henshaw* (Cleary)	Regular school clothes; black construction worker size lunch box. Might stop to open it and the alarm would sound. Could merely carry a large piece of lined cardboard with either "Dear Mr. Henshaw, This year I am in sixth grade." or "A Day on Dad's Rig" printed in large letters on it.
MARCY LEWIS	*The Cat Ate My Gymsuit* (Danziger)	Nothing extraordinary in appearance so interactions have to be focused on. The one with the PE teacher could be chosen:

CHARACTER	AUTHOR AND TITLE(S)	COSTUME, PROP, ACTION, PARTNER, AND DIALOGUE IDEAS
		"Why aren't you playing with the team today?" "Well, the cat ate my gymsuit." Another choice might be the scene with the telephone call from Joel, the boyfriend. Both Marcy's father and Joel would hold telephone receivers. Father would call Marcy: "Marcy, it's your Romeo." Joel would say, when Marcy arrives at the phone, "Hi, Juliet." Marcy would show annoyance and embarrassment.
MARY	*Mary Poppins* (Travers)	Long black coat; black umbrella, opened; carpet bag; hat. Or, she could wear a dress with a white apron and be spooning "medicine" to Michael and Jane from a bottle labelled "One Tea-Spoon to be Taken at Bed-Time." Could depart with an "Au revoir" to the audience.
MR. POPPER	*Mr. Popper's Penguins* (Atwater)	Old fashioned male clothing could be imitated. Absolutely has to be accompanied by at least one penguin. Perhaps the episode where the penguin, on a leash, wraps himself around Mrs. Callahan's legs might be a good one to enact. A model of the rookerie in the refrigerator would be fun to add.
MRS. GORF	*Sideways Stories from Wayside School* (Sachar)	Anything to suggest the stereotype of a "mean teacher"—horn-rimmed spectacles, hair in bun, frown, dowdy clothing, pointer with which to tap and snarl at the audience, "Be quiet or I'll turn you into apples." Should be carrying at least one large bright red apple and turn to smile at it.
MRS. PIGGLE-WIGGLE	*Mrs. Piggle-Wiggle* *Mrs. Piggle-Wiggle's Magic* *Mrs. Piggle-Wiggle's Farm* *Hello, Mrs. Piggle-Wiggle* (MacDonald)	Brown clothing; felt hat; high heels; hair in knot; cookie sheet covered with cookies. Could be joined by Patsy from "The Radish Cure." Patsy might be covered with mud on all visible body parts and be pulling radishes out of a mudpack on her arm; or she could be clean and fresh, holding a plate of red radishes. (Make the radishes larger than life, though.)
MITZI	*Mitzi and the Elephants* (Williams)	Eight-year-old girl; ponytails; skirt; T-shirt with "Support Your Local Zoo" slogan. In representation of the chapter, "The TV Sit Comedy," Mitzi could be jostled by a small boy as three-year-old Darwin. She would

Characters from Fiction

CHARACTER	AUTHOR AND TITLE(S)	COSTUME, PROP, ACTION, PARTNER, AND DIALOGUE IDEAS
		fall and land in a large yellow paper "puddle," registering horror, disgust, and then embarrassment as Darwin reports on the microphone, "Mitzi just fell down and wet her pants." The zebra responsible for the puddle and the adults in the studio could be included. Or, in an alternate choice, zookeeper Ed and Mitzi would walk with the elephants, Cupcake and Daisy, perhaps offering them food. Nana Potts in her frizzy black wig, dangling earrings, square dancing dress, and Adidas could be brandishing a snow scraper at them and Darwin, in pajamas, robe, swim fins, and sunglasses could be belting out his take-off on "Old MacDonald Had a Farm." The animals in both these scenes probably would be best as four-legged ones.
O CRISPIN	*The Champion of Merrimack County* (Drury)	Mouse headgear; "electric blue" crash helmet with "red cockade"; tail with large lump visible in the middle—or splinted and heavily bandaged and supported from a fishing line attached to the helmet. Could be accompanied by Janet Berryfield, carrying an oversize tube of toothpaste, with some toothpaste on her finger ready to be smeared; Janet's mother (in hospital gown?); Janet's father, shaking his head; and any of the other "community helpers." For example, Bangs, the blacksmith, could be included, his prop being a "foot" for the bathtub.
OGDEN PETTIBONE	*The Boy Who Turned into a TV Set* (Manes)	Ordinary school clothing. Voices in falsetto, "I've never seen clothes so clean!" could be utilized (coming from offstage). Ogden would register surprise, look around, and then finally lift up his shirt to expose a picture of a rocket blasting off drawn on his chest. (Appropriate sound effects would be necessary.) Ogden could be accompanied by the TV repair woman (needs toolbox and cap or shirt with TV Service imprint) who would tap on Ogden's head, forehead, and nose with her screwdriver.
OMRI	*The Indian in the Cupboard* (Banks)	Boy in regular school clothing would carry a small white metal cupboard with a keyhole and a mirror, (foil on a painted cardboard box would do) and a key of exaggerated size. The key should have a fancy

CHARACTER	AUTHOR AND TITLE(S)	COSTUME, PROP, ACTION, PARTNER, AND DIALOGUE IDEAS
		head and be suspended from a red satin ribbon. Omri could stop to put a 3″ plastic figure of an Indian on the cupboard shelf or he could be accompanied by another child dressed as the Indian.
OSCAR WINKLE	*Operation: Dump the Chump* (Park)	Oscar, in clothing typical of a 12-year-old, could merely be carrying a sign: "Wanted: Good clean home for helpful young boy. Call 568-6990." He could be carrying a large three-ring notebook, labelled "Secret Notebook" in his other hand. He could also be accompanied by his eight-year-old brother, Robert. Robert might carry a large shoe box in his hand and the scene with the "black widow spiders" from the science lab could be played. Robert would spill the contents of the box; Oscar would be "bitten" and act the distress resulting from his fear of death; and Robert would roll on the floor consumed by laughter.
OTIS	*Otis Spofford* (Cleary)	School clothes. Could be mumbling to himself, "Phooey on that teacher!" while chewing up pieces of paper, wadding them up, and throwing them in a waste basket. Would exit, exclaiming, "Gee, my mouth is dry!"
PETER & JUDY	*Jumanji* (Van Allsburg)	Peter: white shirt and glasses. Judy: braids, jumper and blouse. Should have game box labelled, "Jumanji, a Jungle Adventure Game," with a note taped on it about reading instructions carefully. May be accompanied by the guide in walking shorts and back pack who would look at a map and scratch his head, and/or a group of monkeys tossing plastic dishes at each other. A more ambitious undertaking would include the lion and the herd of rhinos. Providing a big umbrella for the children to huddle under would be a simpler task.
PIPPI	*Pippi Longstocking* *Pippi in the South Seas* *Pippi Goes on Board* (Lindgren)	Carrot pigtails; freckles; long black shoes, twice the size of her feet; 1 brown stocking; 1 black stocking. Could have toy monkey for Mr. Nilsson on her shoulder or another child could represent Mr. Nilsson and wear blue pants, a yellow jacket, and a white straw hat. Pippi might have a rolling pin and "dough" in her hands and roll the dough out on the stage floor, telling Tom-

Characters from Fiction

CHARACTER	AUTHOR AND TITLE(S)	COSTUME, PROP, ACTION, PARTNER, AND DIALOGUE IDEAS
		my and Annika, "This is the way you make cookies." Another option would be to have Pippi carry a half completed drawing of a full size horse accompanied by a teacher, pointer in hand, scolding her.
PONY BOY	*The Outsiders* (Hinton)	My sixth grade girls chose to represent all the Greasers plus Cherry and simply were introduced by character name. They had smudged faces and wore slicked down hair and a variety of clothing, including sweatshirts, black T-shirts, jeans jackets and black leather jackets. Their imitation of the slouching bravado characteristic of the Greasers and of cigarette smoking met with great approval from the audience. Some incidents that could be dramatized would include the confrontation between Randy and Bob, "the Socs", and Two-Bit and Pony Boy about staying away from Soc girls or the skin rumble itself. I would prefer to focus on less violent episodes, however, such as the scene where Johnny cuts Pony Boy's hair with a switch blade, one where Johnny and Pony Boy read *Gone with the Wind*, or the one where Pony Boy is welcomed home by Soda Pop and Darry with a newspaper with the headline "Heroes save kids in burning church" being used as a prop.
PUMPKIN GIANT	*The Pumpkin Giant* (Wilkin)	Orange pumpkin body cover; box head with oversize ugly jack-o'lantern face extending over the edges, mouth open showing jagged teeth. May be joined by king in robe and crown, trembling visibly, and/or Patroclus in ragged clothing, potato in hand ready to be thrown.
RALPH	*The Mouse and the Motorcycle* *Runaway Ralph* *Ralph S. Mouse* (Cleary)	Mouse ears protruding from edge of white plastic bowl helmet; red motorcycle (bicycle will do); tail either tied to handlebar or tucked up under arm. Should be saying "pb-pb-b-b-b." To represent the first title, could carry a large round white disk labelled "aspirin." Could be accompanied by Keith bearing a peanut butter and jelly sandwich.
RAMONA	*Ramona the Pest* *Ramona the Brave*	See also page 71 under Beezus. From *Ramona the Pest* one could choose the fight between Ramona and Howie over posses-

CHARACTER	AUTHOR AND TITLE(S)	COSTUME, PROP, ACTION, PARTNER, AND DIALOGUE IDEAS
	Ramona and her Mother *Ramona and her Father* *Ramona Quimby, Age 8* *Ramona Forever* (Cleary)	sion of the red ribbon Miss Binney had tied around Ramona's old blue rabbit's neck. Or Ramona could be just by herself, riding her trike with one wheel removed, the red ribbon threaded through the spokes of the front wheel. Perhaps the incident that would be the most fun would be from "The Hard-boiled Egg Fad" in *Ramona Quimby, Age 8* where Ramona, a "whacker," smashes her egg against her head and finds out that it is not hard-boiled. Yard Ape, grinning at Ramona, and Marsha, attempting to mother her, could be added.
SAM	*My Side of the Mountain* (George)	Sam could be wearing his two layers of regular clothing—or deerskin—and could carry an ax over his shoulder. He could pause to attempt to build a fire with flint and steel or he might be dangling a "fish" on a hook from his ball of cord. A model to represent Frightful, the falcon, would be ideal.
SOUP	*Soup* *Soup and Me* *Soup for President* *Soup's Drum* *Soup in the Saddle* (Robert Newton Peck)	These titles exude vivid incidents from which to choose. See page 15 and page 119. For students interested in building things, the chapter "Silver Bullet" from *Soup and Me* would be a good choice. Janice Riker and her soapbox racer at which the Silver Bullet was aimed could be included as well as Mrs. Stetson, hitting Janice with a broom, in anger over the destruction in her garden. Janice would point in vain to Soup and Rob as the causative agents in the damage.
TOM	*The Great Brain* *The Great Brain Does It Again* *The Great Brain Reforms* *The Great Brain at the Academy* *The Return of the Great Brain* (Fitzgerald)	Shirt; knickers; freckles. The chapter "The Tin Can Swindle" might be chosen. Tom could wave a can back and forth in front of a spectator's face, saying, "Keep your eyes on the can. Keep your eyes on the can. Count backwards from 10 . . . You are now hypnotised." Or, Tom could wear a new baseball mitt with a baseball in it and be grinning, followed by smaller boys, Jimmie and Danny, complaining, "That's not fair! You tricked us!" If the setting was appropriate, Tom could actually perform the trick. (Directions: pages 29–30 in *The Great Brain Reforms*.)
WILBUR	*Charlotte's Web* (E. B. White)	See pages 115 to 116.

Characters from Fiction

CHARACTER	AUTHOR AND TITLE(S)	COSTUME, PROP, ACTION, PARTNER, AND DIALOGUE IDEAS
WINNIE-THE-POOH	*Winnie-the-Pooh* *The House at Pooh Corner* (A. A. Milne)	Winnie, in bear headgear, could be holding a blue balloon and be humming, "I'm going to get some honey." He could be attended by a bee, in representation of the chapter, "In Which We Are Introduced to Winnie-the-Pooh and Some Bees." He could be accompanied by Christopher Robin, carrying an opened umbrella and saying, "Tut-tut, it looks like rain." Or Winnie could be rubbing his behind and be joined by Christopher Robin carrying his pop gun.

Top: Owl and Tigger, from *The House at Pooh Corner; bottom:* Lion and Tin Woodman, from *The Wizard of Oz.*

VIII. IDEAS FOR CHARACTERS FROM BIOGRAPHY

A SPRINKLING OF CHARACTERS FROM the biography section of the library rounds out a book parade. The representation of these characters does present some problems, however.

First of all, costume makers portraying real people have to pay attention to the entire body. For years I was overwhelmed by this challenge. Both thinking of locating sources for free loans of appropriate clothing and contemplating the construction of white ruffles and fashionable suits from the normal complement of school paper supplies contributed to my discouragement. Furthermore, making up the fresh faces of our young students into some semblance of the visages of our country's adult heroes was also more than my amateur's mind could cope with.

Then, a miracle. I ordered the ALA publication *Storytelling with Puppets*, most ably written by Connie Champlin and Nancy Renfro, and discovered bodi-puppets. Ben Franklin, himself, made from paper and fabric and tied around a child who was holding a "book" labelled "ALMANAC," jumped into my excited view. I found clear directions for making the bodi-puppet (outlined in this book on page 30) and I found that the character's head may be pasted on the flap of the grocery sack, or (why did I not think of this before?!) a box headgear with the face attached may be added. Wonderful! Problem solved.

There are other difficulties in portraying characters from biography, though. One is that characters from biography, even the most famous of these real people, tend to be less distinctive and colorful than the characters that populate our imaginative stories. They are thus more difficult to represent as unique personalities.

I have suggested previously that fictional characters be represented as "larger than life." It is fun to portray Jelly Belly, scoffing down a bagful of jelly donuts, his obesity exaggerated with the use of multiple pillows. It just makes sense to have Harold's purple crayon exaggerated into the length of a yardstick to allow the audience opportunity to see it and make the connection with the character. But the falsity that exaggeration brings to the world of real people, past and present, causes me some distress, even though I realize that a portrayal might be unrecognizable without such overstatement.

Too, there is an inclination to represent the most vivid incident from the biographee's life, even to apocryphal ones. (I think of a possible George Washington dressed as a boy, carrying a cherry tree and hatchet or of a Betsy Ross stitching on the flag.) Such representation, while easily recognizable, would reinforce false stereotypes in the minds of the viewers. As educators, we should be seeking to eliminate falsity rather than encouraging it.

In typifying characters from biography, it is difficult, also, to prevent anachronisms from creeping in. When I show the slide of a student who quite admirably portrayed Abraham Lincoln, complete with tall black hat, gaunt face, beard, white shirt and black suit, the audience howls over his Adidas footwear.

Another consideration in creating figures from biography is the problem of specificity. For example, biographies of sports stars are frequently favored reading from this area of the library. In trying to represent some of these stars, the prop would simply identify the sport, leaving the person indistinguishable. A baseball bat, for example, would be appropriate for George Brett, Roger Maris, and Mickey Mantle, and nothing singularly remarkable from their personal lives could be added. For this dilemma, the team name and uniform colors as well as the player number could be included to allow at least the sports enthusiast to be able to identify and appreciate his or her heroes on parade.

A final caution relates to the atrocities of history. You may share my feeling that the stories of Adolf Hitler and Anne Frank need to be told, but that the characters need not be included in a celebration designed for merry-making. I also try to discourage illustration of battlefield slaughter and violence, whether the source be General Patton or the characters in the ever-popular Star Wars encounters from the fiction section of the library. On the other hand, I can envision a Sadako from Coerr's *Sadako and the Thousand Paper Cranes* making a heart-rending appeal for world peace and of this I heartily approve. It is difficult to be both logical and consistent in decisions based on personal values.

Contemplating the ramifications of some of the problems enumerated above leads me into the statement that probably the best way to enjoy and learn from the offerings of the biography section of the library is to hold a day reserved for these characters alone: a Biography Day or a "Who's Who Party." As described by Elaine K. McEwan in "Practically Speaking," *School Library Journal,* February, 1984, a presentation could consist of more lengthy speeches from the characters themselves rather than the short introductions necessitated by a parade. A variation, the choice of which might be influenced by the exigencies of large class sizes and short audience spans, would be to pair students, using one as the interviewer of the biographee in a dialogue format. This approach would allow for participation from each student, shorten the presentation, and liven the action. Another alternative would be the utilization of the biography characters, within the classroom, in a guessing game that would extend over several days, allowing all class members to take part and be the center of attention. This game, written up as "Students as mystery guests" in the May/June 1986 issue of *Learning Magazine,* basically consists of a twenty- (or fewer) question situation with "yes" or "no" answers narrowing down the identity assumed by the student, who does not necessarily have to be in costume.

Without the structure of a Biography Day and even before the inspiration of the bodipuppet idea, however, one year at my school a team of five characters popped into classrooms with very brief introductions of themselves to successfully bring to the students' attention the historical contributions of women in celebration of Women's History Week.

Susan B. Anthony, with her hair in a bun, tiny wire spectacles, shawl, long dress, and poster from TABS, said, with some asperity in her voice:

> George Washington helped win the vote for fewer than 2 million white males. Abraham Lincoln helped win the vote for fewer than 1 million black males. But I, Susan B. Anthony, helped win the vote for 26 million American women!*

Amelia Earhart looked authentic wearing a jump suit, a flying white neck scarf, and aviation headgear represented by a bathing cap and goggles. Wilma Rudolph, the first American woman to win three Olympic gold medals, ran in, wearing sweatband and track clothing and simulating the panting she would be doing at the end of a race. Madame Curie, appropriately dressed for her time period, carried a test tube and beaker and spoke of the physical difficulties under which she had conducted her scientific work. Finally, a prototype pioneer woman of the nineteenth-century westward movement listed in poetic fashion the many tasks that were hers. Unfortunately our planned Harriet Tubman was not able to join the group.

In addition, our Erie parades have rather consistently included someone dressed in ragged shirt, trousers tied around the waist with a rope, hobo stick with kerchief bundle over the shoulder, small sack containing popcorn "seeds" in hand, kitchen pot on the head. Johnny (Chapman) Appleseed has been portrayed by both teachers and students. Although the costuming evokes Walt Disney's image of Johnny Appleseed, I seem to relax my objections to film creations for this one character.

It *is* possible, then, to include characters from the realm of biography in a parade situa-

---

*Quote from TABS Susan B. Anthony poster © 1977 Organization for Equal Education of the Sexes, Inc., 438 Fourth St., Brooklyn, NY 11215. Used by permission.

Abraham Lincoln

Johnny Appleseed

tion. The following is a small sampling from the selection available. (Incidentally, although not listed, a current "hot" rock star, if his or her biography is available in your library, would be much appreciated, particularly by the older students.)

PERSON	COSTUME, PROP, ACTION, PARTNER IDEAS
HANK AARON	Baseball uniform and bat; no. 44 on shirt; *A* on cap for Atlanta Braves (although he did end his career with the Milwaukee Brewers). Could carry a big sign, "755 home runs"; or, he could pantomime a big hit, (not using a ball), and shout, "That's my record home run! 755! Yippee!!" as he shades his eyes to look into the distant sky.
KAREEM ABDUL JABBAR (Lew Alcindor)	Basketball uniform; L.A. Lakers identification; basketball. Could be dribbling ball and pretend to shoot a basket and then stop to announce proudly. "That makes _____ points! I'm the leading scorer in the NBA." (The current figure is over 31,419 points for Kareem.)
MUHAMMAD ALI (Cassius Clay)	Boxing shorts and gloves; hightop sneakers. Introduction as the Heavyweight Boxing Champion or sign to that effect carried by another student. Could prance with appropriate footwork and then stop, arms overhead, gloves touching in a victory gesture and shout, "I am the greatest!"
SUSAN B. ANTHONY	See page 86.
NEIL ARMSTRONG	Ski clothes or jump suit for space suit; back pack; boots; helmet; U.S. flag in hand. Could hold sign, "Apollo 11, July, 1969," and take a big jump, pretending to plant the flag. Or could show a picture of his footprint on the moon's surface and say, "That's one small step for a man, one giant leap for mankind."
CLARA BARTON	Long dress; boots; apron; soup pot. Could be attending a soldier with a bandaged head or arm, blood showing through the bandages, of course, accompanied by a microphone introduction of her as the "Angel of the Battlefield." Or, she could be simply wearing a dressy long dress and carry a placard showing a large red cross.
ALEXANDER GRAHAM BELL	Long coat. Should carry telephone. (Consult reference books for purposes of authentic replication.) Would say through the instrument, "Mr. Watson, come here, I want you." This could be prefaced perhaps by his spilling some pretend battery acid on his clothing.
JOHN CHAPMAN (Johnny Appleseed)	See pages 86–87. Costume could include patches pinned on his trousers and student could wear bare feet. Could be also carrying a Bible tucked into the top of his pants.

Characters from Biography

PERSON	COSTUME, PROP, ACTION, PARTNER IDEAS
CHRISTOPHER COLUMBUS	Tights, tunic with sash; puffed breeches. Might be most effectively done by means of a bodi-puppet. Could carry a Spanish flag on a standard or could hold two pictures, one showing a flat earth with a ship falling off the edge, the other showing a round earth with the continents as envisioned by Columbus. He would shake his head over the former, and nod approvingly as he looked at the latter. Another child could precede Columbus and display the sign, "1492." A backdrop of a ship, labelled the *Santa Maria*, would add to the presentation. Columbus could also be accompanied by a sailor, dressed in rolled up jeans or cotton pants, wearing a scarf wrapped around his head and tied in the back, sandals on his feet, and a coil of rope over his arm. The sailor would shade his eyes to peer over the sea, point excitedly, and call out "Land ho!"
JACQUES COUSTEAU	Knitted cap; curved pipe; casual clothing; scuba or aqua lung equipment or video camera. Presentation could include a backdrop of undersea life or a model of Cousteau's diving saucer.
MARIE CURIE (Madame Curie)	See page 86. A second student could be pushing a wheelbarrow heaped with rocks and labelled, "Uranium Ore."
WALT DISNEY	White-shirted, modern day dress; moustache; large sketch of Mickey Mouse and paint brush held in hand. A backdrop of the gates or a notable part of Disneyland would be nice. Could be accompanied by a Snow White, singing, "Some day my Prince will come. . . ."
AMELIA EARHART	See page 86. Could be carrying a sign printed with either "1897–1937?" or "First woman to fly across the Atlantic."
THOMAS EDISON	Suit with bow tie. Could carry an oversize model of a light bulb or a chemistry set. In the case of the latter prop, a student wearing a cap labelled, "Conductor," might be boxing his ears and shoving him. He could carry a cylinder covered with foil from which would lead a tube and a funnel and be reciting, "Mary had a little lamb" into the funnel.
LEIF ERIKSON	Tunic; Viking headgear and shield; sword; footwear with crisscross strap up leg. A backdrop of a Viking ship might be included.

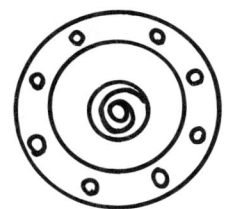 

PERSON	COSTUME, PROP, ACTION, PARTNER IDEAS
BENJAMIN FRANKLIN	Could be costumed as a boy with his thumbs in holes in two boards as described in Graves' biography. He would be accompanied by his peers, laughing at Ben's "swimming machine." More stereotypically, he might appear as a man, carrying a kite and a large key. In this case, he might be accompanied by a person carrying a jagged model of lightning, sound effects might be provided, and Ben could recoil from the force of the lightning. A third alternative would be to dress him as a man with a bald head, wearing the glasses associated with his image, and a suit with a ruffle up its front. (A bodi-puppet would be the quickest way to costume here.) Here Ben would carry a large mock-up of a book entitled, *Poor Richard's Almanac*, in addition to a quill feather. See page 30.
HARRY HOUDINI	Bathing trunks; rope ties; chains with padlocks; handcuffs. A large version of one of the posters advertising his feats could be included.
THOMAS JEFFERSON	Knee britches; stockings; suit coat; slip or lace handkerchief neck ruffle with brooch; or bodi-puppet incorporating all the preceding. Would hold a large sheet of paper clearly headed, "Declaration of Independence," or use a facsimile of the real article perhaps available in the library's vertical file. He might stop to begin a speech: "We hold these truths to be self-evident, that all men are created equal." A backdrop of Monticello would be a plus.
HELEN KELLER	Long dress; a copy of *The Story of My Life* in enlarged size. Could be "looking" with a sightless gaze or using her fingers to touch another lady's nose and lips, positioning her thumb on the lady's larynx as Helen was accustomed to doing. She could be costumed as a little girl in a pinafore and have a temper tantrum. The temper tantrum could be smoothed over by another lady in long dress who takes Helen's hand and does finger spelling (Annie Sullivan).
MARTIN LUTHER KING, JR.	Black choir gown or cape to ankles; mortarboard on head; Nobel Peace Prize "pin" on chest; sign, "I have a dream" as Eisner suggests. An alternate idea would be for the student to enclose himself in a box, made into a replica of a prison cell and carried by its bars. It might be labelled "Birmingham." The student could take the time to make the following speech with appropriate gestures and with emotion evident in his voice: I have a dream that one day this nation will rise up and live out the true meaning of its creed, "We hold these truths to be self-evident; that all men are created equal."

Characters from Biography

PERSON	COSTUME, PROP, ACTION, PARTNER IDEAS
ABRAHAM LINCOLN	Top hat; black suit or cape; string tie; beard; Gettysburg Address printed in large letters on a sheet in his hand. Again, a speech might be in order: Four score and seven years ago our fathers brought forth, upon this continent, a new nation, conceived in Liberty, and dedicated to the proposition that all men are created equal.
CHARLES LINDBERGH	Fur-collared windbreaker; trousers tucked into knee socks; aviation headgear (bathing cap and goggles will do); sign: "New York to Paris, 1927." Could also have a cardboard model of a plane labelled, "Spirit of St. Louis."
FLORENCE NIGHTINGALE	Long dress; shawl; nurse's cap, lantern. Could be giving water to a soldier who thanks the "Lady of the Light."
SALLY RIDE	Jump suit; NASA designation and Sally's name on the left front of the suit; motorcycle helmet; sign, "First woman in space, 1983." Could also carry an illustration of the *Challenger*.
PETE ROSE	Baseball uniform; bat; #14 on the uniform; "Red" on the shirt pocket; "Rose" on the shirt back. Could demonstrate switch-hitting (from either side) and/or pretend to slide into a base with a belly flop. Could boast, "I beat Ty Cobb's hitting record!" or hold a sign saying, "4,192 hits!!" or "Champion Hitter!"
SACAGAWEA	Cape of fringed burlap or grocery bags; braids; plain kerchief over head; paper bag moccasins or white socks worn as boots; doll in papoose holder on back. Could be leaning on a stick, pointing out a direction to Lewis and Clark, both in long-sleeved fringed outfits, boots, fur hats, and carrying rifles. Signs could communicate, "To the Pacific!" or simply, "The Lewis and Clark Expedition."
O. J. SIMPSON	Football uniform; Buffalo Bills #32. Could carry a Heisman trophy or a glass of orange juice. Again, a sign or a boast: "2,003 yards!"
SQUANTO	Wig with long braided hair; headband with feather; deerskin shirt and trousers fabricated from grocery bag material, crumpled and then flattened; breech cloth; moccasins. A bodi-puppet would work nicely. Could carry some fish and a stalk of corn and could be accompanied by a Pilgrim.
HARRIET TUBMAN	Long skirt; shawl; sign: "To Canada." Might use a finger over her lips to indicate "Shh!" and be beckoning the advance of some people, acting as though stealthily treading through the forest in a semi-crouched position. The addition of a chicken,

PERSON	COSTUME, PROP, ACTION, PARTNER IDEAS
	either real or costumed, and an overseer of slaves with a whip would allow for a dramatization of the way Harriet tricked the plantation administrators as described in the biography by Epstein.
GEORGE WASHINGTON	Tri-cornered hat; lace handkerchief with brooch at throat; short overcoat; knee britches; high boots; or bodi-puppet. Could be accompanied by soldiers in ragged and torn farmer clothing, shivering, and holding a Valley Forge sign.
WRIGHT BROTHERS (Orville and Wilbur)	Regular male clothing; airmen's peaked caps. Could carry a kite and a sign, "Kittyhawk, Dec. 17, 1903." Could carry a model of the plane they used possibly made from styrofoam meat trays and toothpicks or be lugging a wind tunnel, a long box with a fan at one end and tiny airplane models at the other.

IX. A FEW NOTES ON NON-FICTION

MORE THAN CONTENT WITH THE innumerable marvelous characters available for gleaning from folk and fictional literature, I seem to have no need to look further into non-fiction. In fact, I confess to have somewhat of an antipathy toward the non-fiction that has found its way into representation at Erie School parades.

I confess to not being terribly enthusiastic about the third grader in his soccer uniform, soccer ball in hand, illustrating *The Soccer Book*. I confess that I wished that the talented fifth grade artist who produced a beautiful poster of a butterfly in representation of *The How and Why Wonder Book of Butterflies and Moths*, instead would have presented *herself* as the beautiful butterfly into which Carle's hungry caterpillar was transformed. And I confess that the sixth grader's float with models of tanks and artillery used in World War II left me cold.

Still, in spite of my prejudiced view, I *can* see some areas of non-fiction beyond folklore and biography that would be a source for titles that would fit into my vision of a book *character* celebration. Perhaps a further exploration would be profitable.

Mythology is a fruitful field. I would love to see Pegasus and Icarus in flight during a parade. Certainly a Medusa would cause a sensation, as would Cyclops. Persephone, with her pomegranate half eaten, I would welcome as I would Atlas himself, with the world on his shoulders. The list from this classification is quite extensive.

Old Testament characters could also be included. A David, for example, in an off-shoulder tunic and carrying a slingshot, could be accompanied by another student with an extremely large stick puppet head, as Goliath. This student could fall as David pantomimes the use of the slingshot.

Another rich source of memorable characters is the poetry section of the library. The Queen of Eene[2], for instance, just cries out to materialize in flesh at a parade. With her crown on upside down, her queenly robes flowing behind her, and a cut onion and toothbrush in her grasp, she would sob disarmingly about her lack of visitors.

Many other characters created by the fertile imaginations of Jack Prelutsky and Shel Silverstein deserve attention. Some come to mind, instantly:

> Cecil Snedde, with his red nose and seven sneezes,
> "The Seven Sneezes of Cecil Snedde"[3]
>
> Dainty Dottie Dee, with her lathered spaghetti,
> "Dainty Dottie Dee"[1]
>
> Deaf Donald, with his "I love you" signing,
> "Deaf Donald"[4]
>
> Jimmy Jet, turned into a TV set,
> "Jimmy Jet and his TV Set"[5]
>
> Lazy Jane, with her mouth open, waiting for a drink of water,
> "Lazy Jane"[5]
>
> The Loser, with his head as a seat,
> "The Loser"[5]

Mr. Spats, with twenty-two hats,
"Mr. Smeds and Mr. Spats"[4]

Mrs. McTwitter, sitting on the baby,
"Sitter"[4]

Peggy Ann McKay, with her illnesses,
"Sick"[5]

Sarah Cynthia Sylvia Stout, with her garbage
"Sarah Cynthia Sylvia Stout Would Not Take the Garbage Out"[5]

Nor should we overlook Mudville's Casey, Lear's old man with the collection of birds nesting in his beard, or even Robert Louis Stevenson's shadow. And I would not forget "The Owl and the Pussy-Cat." I would also consult *Poem Stew* on the Reading Rainbow shelf and come up with William Cole's "Sneaky Pete" among others. Again, the list is extensive enough to consider for a festival and/or parade based on poetry alone. (See Jane Robertson's and Beth Alvin's "Practically Speaking," *School Library Journal*, August 1985, page 34, for just that.)

Leaving mythology and poetry to move to the applied science classification, I can readily see, for example, that students would really enjoy building one of the creations from Jim Murphy's *Weird and Wacky Inventions*. At the same time, however, I am conscious that I really view the representation of this type of book as belonging to the book talk or book commercial program of the library rather than to a book character celebration. I may be wrong. I *could* merely drop the word "character" from my celebration name. A production from Murphy's book *would* make a very visually effective parade entry, depending on the invention selected, and certainly would be a great advertisement for the book. (And somehow, I do recall that providing such advertisement was a prime motivation for parade efforts.) In addition, although I hate to admit it, perhaps there are those students who will *never* relate to fictional characters but who *will* read and enjoy non-fiction. Obviously, I have some difficulty in following through on my preference for the exclusion of the major portion of non-fiction from a book character celebration.

In final comment, I will add that I have similar ambivalent feelings about representation of books from the 900 classification. Although the most spectacular book parade float I have ever seen was produced by a first grade class based on the title, *Mexico from A to Z* (call number 917.2, and although I would be one of the first to support any possibility of the promotion of world peace through an increase in the understanding of various cultures, my choice, once more, would be to assist in this promotion at a time other than that designated for a celebration of book characters from children's literature. Your choice may well be different.

Notes

1. Prelutsky, Jack. *The New Kid on the Block*. Greenwillow, 1984.

2. Prelutsky, Jack. *The Queen of Eene*. Greenwillow, 1978.

3. Prelutsky, Jack. *The Sheriff of Rottenshot*. Greenwillow, 1982.

4. Silverstein, Shel. *A Light in the Attic*. Harper & Row, 1981.

5. Silverstein, Shel. *Where the Sidewalk Ends*. Harper & Row, 1974.

X. WHAT TO DO WITH A COSTUMED BOOK CHARACTER; OR, PUTTING ON A CELEBRATION

A POSSIBLE RESPONSE TO THE QUESTION, "What do you do with a costumed book character?" is, "Nothing!" This answer is not quite as tongue-in-cheek as you might expect. I might amend it to read, less succinctly, "Nothing but enjoy the character."

Book Character Costume Day

I could see, with the support of a book-oriented faculty, that a school-wide Book Character Day with no formally scheduled functions might be the choice of the librarian interested in making a start at celebrating books with costumed characters. Indeed, such a day might be the choice at any time for the pleasure it brings.

For children (and teachers) to see the principal in his bathrobe and stocking cap, candle holder in hand, representing Jack from Mother Goose, is sheer delight.

Hearty chuckles greeted the arrival at school of my library clerk dressed as Ralph from *The Mouse and the Motorcycle* on such a Book Character Costume Day. The plumpish, grey-haired lady, wearing mouse ears larger than dinner plates and pushing a bicycle along the school corridors, became more dearly beloved than ever.

Meanwhile, the school custodian was doubling over with loud guffaws at my long, brown Katy kangaroo tail—and my hop. I, in turn, was admiring the second grade teacher, dressed in youthful clothing and flat shoes and wearing a straw hat on which a large pipe cleaner spider was situated. When I saw that the adorable stuffed animal under her arm was a pig, I knew instantly who she was. The pleasure snowballed with the recognition of each new character and a festive camaraderie prevailed.

Unquestionably, aside from the fun, one big advantage of holding a Book Character Costume Day is the inclusiveness of the celebration. All students have the opportunity to participate.

Even though no formal presentation would be scheduled, within each classroom, introductions of the characters to schoolmates could take place. Or, times could be set aside for students, a grade level at a time, to wend their way through the corridors in order to be viewed. An alternate approach, requiring more planning in its execution, is one used by a school librarian in my district. (See page 100.)

However, granting the positive attributes of a Book Character Costume Day, I might still opt for other kinds of presentations of book characters. For one reason, some other kinds of presentations provide opportunity for the students to make meaningful, planned, and practiced oral presentations. For another, some presentations provide more specific focus on titles and character names, thus better publicizing the offerings of the library collection.

Finally, although not necessarily so, when the entire school participates in a costume day, preparation is usually done at home. In this situation, students from less privileged homes frequently do not have adequate resources for participation in the celebration. In addition, many students appear in ready-made Halloween costumes and renditions of TV and movie characters which have little to do with reading books. Illegible signs and other problems of costume execution show up, also.

Use of some classroom time for guidance from the teacher regarding character choice and communication of "essence" would alleviate the above-mentioned problems. Time for complete costume preparation in the classroom using school supplies would eliminate them.

Formalized Presentations

Single Class Presentation

As a classroom teacher by yourself, with no school-wide support for a book celebration, can you justify taking the amount of "teaching time" necessary to prepare for and participate in a formal book character presentation? I hope that your answer is a resounding, "Yes!"

In case you need to be persuasive with a textbook-oriented administrator, you might point out the necessary comprehension and writing skills that will be put to use in the creation of the students' sentences related to the character, not to mention the thought that will go into the planning of the costume. You might stress the enhancement both of oral language skills and self-confidence through the practice that is a requisite for speaking with expression before an audience. Finally, you might emphasize the increased motivation for reading. Books about which some students have never heard may be the ones selected and illustrated by their classmates, and certainly, if the presentations are done well, they will tempt further investigation of the titles. (See also pages 97 and 102 for other gains possible from the learning experience.)

Cognizant of all these benefits available to children, you as a single classroom teacher will want to go ahead on your own with a book character celebration or proselytize other teachers into joining you. It is a relatively simple matter to invite another class, either on your grade level or below, to visit your classroom for a presentation. On the other hand, knowing the disorder likely to occur in the room when a large number of children get costumed, it just might be better to visit the invited class's room.

Of course, a request to room parents for some help with the actual pinning and tying on the day of the presentation would be a good idea, too.

During the visit to a selected classroom, it would be appropriate for an announcer to indicate, in enthusiastic tones, "In honor of National Children's Book Week we are proud to present some characters directly from the pages of books in our library."

Entrances from the hallway, one at a time, make for a more interesting program, producing some suspense for the audience as well as providing freedom from the distraction of the appearance of several characters at one time. In turn, then, each character would introduce himself or herself, making known both the character name and the book title associated with the character. Ideally, for purposes of advertising, the actual book should be shown also. In addition, one facet of the character, chosen to be of maximum interest to the audience, could be summarized in a sentence or two. For example: "Hi, I'm Harold from *Harold and the Purple Crayon* and I draw wonderful mountains and moons. I have *so* much fun climbing on all the things I draw! Oops! I just tripped over a star!!" And Harold would fall. Or, "Hello, I'm George from the book, *George and Martha*, and I'm feeling very sad today because I fell while I was roller skating and I broke off my favorite tooth." And he would hold up a white cardboard tooth with a sob.

The addition of a little dramatic action or some brief dialogue between two characters will make the presentation all the more entertaining. Harold could crash to the floor with his arms flailing or he could prolong the falling, as though going through a distance in space,

Putting on a Celebration

pretend to use his oversize purple crayon to draw a pillow, and finally land on a real pillow surreptitiously supplied by a classmate. Or, George could be joined by Martha with a plateful of chocolate chip cookies which she would offer to George to cheer him up. Or, George could break down into prolonged sobbing. Martha might put her arm around him, pat his back, and say, "There, there, George. You will look so handsome with a *gold* tooth instead." George would reply, brightening a little, "Do you think so. Martha?" Martha would reassure, "Of course, George." The sketch could conclude with a grateful and resigned George thanking Martha or with the actual attachment of the gold tooth.

After the individual presentation, if space permitted, the character(s) would move to one side and sit quietly, yielding the spotlight to the next individual or group. However, if the classroom is a typical one in size, an exit may be necessary. An alternate plan might be to book time for the use of auditorium or cafeteria space.

The speeches and dramatizations do require many dry runs before the actual day of the costumed presentation. Not a great deal of classroom time has to be taken, however, since practice before small groups of children can yield a splendid number of ideas for improvement from the children themselves (practice in critical thinking), while you, the teacher can be working with another group focusing on a totally different area of the curriculum.

At least one rehearsal must be made in front of the entire class, however, to ensure that the spoken lines are audible to someone at the rear of the room. At this time, students need to be cautioned that, with headgear in place, they will have to speak even more loudly. In fact, a volume they might use to call from the sidelines to a friend involved in a soccer game could be recommended.

Although the costumed book celebrations are a popular activity choice, not all students in the class will be at a high enough level of confidence in themselves to be enthusiastic about a required assignment for participation. I would have a tendency to firmly urge everyone in the class to participate, knowing that, if not during the production, then afterwards, the pleasurable feeling of a job well done will be a great boost to self-assurance. I would have an equally strong tendency, notwithstanding, to suggest an alternate assignment with fewer emotional demands for the child who is obviously not ready for finding such a performance before an audience to be a positive experience.

One way in which to lessen the pain of "being on stage" is to plan the presentation for a younger audience rather than for peers. In such a case, the emphasis would be on those stories with which the younger students would be most interested.

The choice of a younger audience yields benefits other than the enhancement of the comfort factor. Here is a wonderful way to make it socially acceptable for a fifth grader who reads, say, at second grade level, to check out *Danny and the Dinosaur* from the school library. He or she will be able to relish the success of being able to read a library book without any chance of derision from classmates. Indeed, using such "baby books" for the book character festivities could ease such a youngster into a longer term use of readers appropriate for his or her ability, particularly if, following the program, the teacher could set up a continuing "reading buddy" partnership with a student from the lower grades.

Incidentally, let it not be thought that such presentations may only be given by students in the upper grades. Last year, the first grade classes at my school visited the kindergarten classes and every first grader participated in the celebration and each had a speaking part.

An alternate method of presentation of costumed book characters to a class, one that increases the viewers' enjoyment, is the use of a guessing game format. Books would be hidden; all characters would enter the classroom at the same time; and students in the audience, as permitted by the student master of ceremonies, would guess the characters' names. As each is guessed correctly, the character would step forward, bow or curtsy, and then launch into the prepared speech and/or dramatization. The teacher (or student announcer, if sophisticated enough) does need to be alert to the timing necessary to ease out of incorrect guesses with some verbal clues as to the real identity of the character before feelings are hurt. Or, in anticipation of some inability to name the character, each student who will be on stage can be prepared ahead of time to present a short clue, verbal or otherwise, as to his or her identity. Again, if it becomes obvious that the viewers are unacquainted with the book in question after the clue is given, the teacher needs to be ready to interject with an exclamation about the book's merits and with praise for the student's portrayal of the character. "Oh, I can tell that you haven't met the neat characters in *Strega Nona* yet. "_____ [student's name] makes a marvelous Big Anthony. He has had to eat so much pasta . . . you can see how fat his tummy is . . . (and the lead-in to the student's sentences) . . . Big Anthony, why have you eaten so much spaghetti?"

At the conclusion of the presentation it would seem appropriate for the announcer to let the audience know that the books will be available to them for check out from the school library. In fact, on the way back to the home classroom, a stop at the library could be made to leave the books as well as headgear and props suitable for display. A special scheduling of the visited class for a library period shortly following the publicity would also make sense.

Exchange Presentations

Visits to single classrooms are just one way of presenting book characters. Even better are exchange visits planned between two classrooms, following the principle, "The more, the merrier."

The celebration itself could be extended to two days. Or, breaking down the class into small groups, five or six students from each classroom could make the presentations every day over a week's time. This method of scheduling relieves the strain resulting from all the students in a class getting into costumes at the same time.

Tours

A way of reaching an even greater number of viewers would be to hold a pop-in tour throughout the entire school. Ten characters at a time, or fewer, would visit each classroom in turn, covering the whole school.

Particular attention must be paid to timing for such a tour. The various recess schedules as well as the times of special classes such as PE and music have to be taken into consideration. I have made sure that teachers are aware of the approximate time frame of these pop-in visits in order to allow them to adjust their day's lesson planning. In addition, since not all teachers welcome an interruption in their classroom routine, I have always circulated a form beforehand, making it easy for those who prefer no diversions and distractions in their classrooms to decline the visit. (See Appendix A, page 126.)

For these school-wide pop-in tours, each student would introduce himself or herself, as described under the heading, "Single Class Presentations."

In a less formal manner, book characters may be presented to greater numbers of students than is possible with a single class presentation by scheduling quick tours of the cafeteria and/or the playground. In this instance, the various groups may make periodic stops so that children may examine the costumes and engage in some casual guessing as to the identities of the characters.

One year I had three or four costumed library aides circulate around the playground before school, remaining completely silent when questions were asked of them or when conjectures as to the characters they represented were made. A notice read on the school's morning P.A. announcements, however, stated that the first class to identify the book characters on the playground that morning and send the names to the office immediately following

Putting on a Celebration

the announcements would be congratulated during the following day's bulletins. I would be remiss if I did not divulge that there was a slight problem in the execution of this plan. Students tended to kill each other getting through the office door on that and on subsequent mornings during book week.

Assembly Presentations

A more formal, and more stress-producing way for the classroom teacher or librarian to go is to plan a presentation for an all-school assembly. I have found, however, that the delight of both library aides and most of the student body in the occasion has more than compensated for the tension.

I have usually used the Cat in the Hat, portrayed by either sex, as a master of ceremonies, having him prance to the front of the assembled group to the Pink Panther tune provided by the music teacher on the piano and cheer for himself and books. Sometimes, he rudely interrupts the principal in mid sentence by tapping him on the shoulder after sneaking up. After an explanation of the celebration he gives a lead-in suggestive of the identity of the character about to step through the library door, which is facing the patio where the audience is grouped.

Prior to the assembly, the door has been framed by jagged points of colored paper and has been covered with butcher paper on which has been printed an excerpt from a well-known book. At the last minute I slit the butcher paper with a knife to allow the first character to exit from the library without tearing the whole thing down. Incidentally, the entrances are made from a platform inside the library to a stage on the other side of the doorway, utilized to maximize visualization of the character.

A member of the school band provides a drum roll or the music teacher plays appropriate music; the character steps on stage and engages in a verbal exchange with the Cat in the Hat; the M.C. dismisses the character: "Now Goldilocks, don't you go into any more houses in the woods without being invited! O.K.?" after Goldilocks perhaps sobs about the broken chair in her hands; and the character steps off to applause to clear the stage for the next performer. More drama has been supplied on some occasions with Goldilocks making a running departure as a student, dressed as Baby Bear and planted in the audience, screeches, "Someone has been sleeping in my bed and there she is!!"

The Cat in the Hat continues, perhaps with a, "Well, folks, Goldilocks was rather upset. . . . Let's see if we have a happier book character for you behind these pages." He peers through the tear in the paper and says, "Oh, there you are! . . . Ladies and gentlemen, may I present the famous . . ." as out comes Curious George, sporting his medal, and proud as a peacock over it. And so on.

When the end is reached (and I have had approximately 10–15 characters for such an event), all characters crowd back onto the stage with the Cat in the Hat to sing a song to the tune of "Twinkle, Twinkle, Little Star."

> We are, we are, your friends from books,
> Hope that you liked our looks.
> When you visit the library, [li-brar-y]
> Look us up, we don't cost a fee.
> Now join with us in a big, "Hoo-ray,"
> That's how we feel about books today.

The program concludes with the Cat in the Hat leading the audience and characters in three cheers for books. (See Appendix C, pages 136–144 for typical scripts.)

Parades

Although I tend to groan over the tension this method of presenting costumed book characters creates in me, on every occasion that I have coordinated parades, but one, I have enjoyed the results. The exception? In an inner city school, the children and teachers were motivated to enter the parade by the offering of prizes, as, for example, an ice cream party for the winning classroom entry. The contestants, and that is what they were, paraded before judges in addition to the regular school viewers. The judges made evaluations as to first, second, and third place standings in various categories. Competition was fierce; individual characters and floats were creative and well executed; and judges were efficient. But the librarian was unhappy with having exuberant, vaunting winners, and disappointed, downhearted losers, especially when the lines of differentiation as to quality were very difficult to draw. The result appeared to me to be the antithesis of what I had aimed for. I *had* been interested in holding a gala merrymaking that would be enjoyed by all participants and that would generate happy feelings about books and reading.

I vowed that no more judging would be done for book parades that I would coordinate. My emphasis would be on the celebration rather than on the competition. If I do give awards, each participant receives a certificate or an "Honor Participant" blue ribbon and everyone is a winner. Some years I have written "Happy-gram" notes to each class having entries, individualizing the notes to mention details of each child's appearance.

I realize that not all would share my distaste for judged awards, however. You should know that a colleague in my school district has been conducting very successful Book Character Costume Days at her school, ending in an assembly at which judging takes place among candidates preselected from each classroom. If you do decide to have your students' efforts judged, you may want to look over the categories used at my fellow librarian's school. They include the following:

 Biography
 Fairy Tale
 Fiction
 Most Unusual Animal
 Most Unique
 Most Elegant
 Most Weird

She reports that the judges choose one winner from the primary grades and one winner from the upper grades for each of the categories above.

Some members of the audience, in addition to participants, earned awards in Janice Sherick's Storybook Character Parade held during a February "Love of Reading Week." Her nineteen costumed characters, one submitted per class, paraded at an assembly program while a clue to each character's identity was read. In most cases, a passage from the book served as the clue. Later, students filled out ballots with their guesses as to the name of each of the characters after viewing their photographs on display. Best guessers at primary and intermediate levels received prizes. Incidentally, Sherick advised that she would likely publish a list of the characters and their books on a future occasion "so that the students would have an easier time" with their guesses.

In addition to the decision about the kinds of awards to be given for the parade participant, the parade coordinator has to make a decision about the means of limiting the number of entries per class. This necessity has made me want to encourage inter-class exchanges over a parade so that a greater number of students may participate and so that each may have a chance to speak before an audience.

Putting on a Celebration

Nevertheless, teachers at my school have tended to request parades. Thus, I have found myself listing participation-limiting rules:

Not more than *three* (or five, depending on how ambitious I was feeling at the time of writing) entries per class.

Not more than ten students or one third of the class actively parading making up these entries.

(See typical entry forms, Appendix B, pages 132–135).

My concerns, of course, have been

1. that an audience must be left to view and appreciate the parade, in addition to parent viewers;
2. that the parade should be not longer than the spectators' attention span.

Our Erie parades, incidentally, have usually had about 150–200 student participants out of a total school population of 600. In the light of my second concern, I would like to limit a parade to 100 participants since I do include very brief introductions for each.

In the past our parades have worked like this. I have had each classroom's "library rep" (or student council members or library club members on different occasions) wear a distinctive announcer hat. (They have varied from simple construction paper fold-overs to styrofoam barbershop quartet boaters, purchased from a costume supply company.) The announcer goes to the microphone and introduces each entry from the class using the character name rather than the child's name. The parade people group in the cafeteria and exit through the door as they are introduced. The provision of a stage has been helpful in allowing better viewing of the characters by the onlookers assembled in the grassy patio. After the introduction and the bow, curtsy, pantomime, or brief skit, the characters go to an area behind the classrooms to have their pictures taken while awaiting the parade itself. After the entire group has been introduced, the school band contributes some lively marching tunes and the parade is on. I encourage the participants to "ham it up," both on the stage and throughout the parade itself. Fat Jelly Belly cramming in big mouthfuls of food, Doctor De Soto offering applications from his bottle of glue to individuals in the audience, the funny little woman running in fear from the wicked *oni*, and Old King Cole simply looking jolly, all add spice to the festivities.

A few years ago, it became clear to me that the library reps, children ranging in age from 6 to 12, had varying degrees both of confidence and of ability to project their voices. It also became clear that, in the strain of the event itself, they frequently forgot all the training practice pointers that had been emphasized. Thus, in latter years, I have held announcer tryouts for the 6th grade library aides. (See Appendix C for a Cat in the Hat tryout speech.) Normally, about 15 students try for the coveted Cat in the Hat role in the upcoming celebration. After that difficult choice is made, others of the interested volunteers are worked into announcer, special book character, and/or stage crew positions. The chosen announcers and I work together on possible introductions for and/or dialogue with characters in the parade, have intensive practice with the microphone, and finally a non-costumed practice with the characters themselves. It has worked well to have each announcer responsible for the entries from one grade level. Accompanied by a drum roll, he or she bows, flourishing his or her hat to indicate the end of the grade level entries and the time for applause.

Library Club announcers and troubleshooter.

Gratifying responses for the effort involved in coordinating a parade—and meaningful language arts exercises—have been the letters written to me from children in the audience. A sampling follows:

Dear Mrs Wilson   11-19-82

I liked the Wizzard of Oz the best. I liked the dog lady. I liked E.T. to. Thank you for leting us come to the book parade. Chris and Cindy and Mechile and Kendra were in it.

Your friend Brien

Putting on a Celebration

11/19/82

Dear Mrs. Wilson:

I sure liked the parad. I an sure glad we have you for a libriayin.

you had a nice jump. thank you for this book parad day. it was neat.

you'r Admre. Emory

(It was neat)

11-19-82

Dear Mrs. Wilson,

I relly liked the prade your costme was the best but I still liked all of the other ones I hope we can do it again sometime

Love Stephanie S.

Putting on a Celebration

The student reporter for the school newspaper also did some writing about the parade.

Book Parade
   By Marcy Thomas

The sky was blue, the sun was shining, fluffy little clouds floated across the sky setting the scene for the 1983 Book Parade at Erie School. And this year the Book Parade was really great. Some of the costumes I thought were neat were .... The Outsiders by Jennifer Lunt, Kendall Milford, Sharla Carson, Sandra Cons, Tonya Regoli and Darian Knoblock. Jelly Belly by Traci Coates and Darby Johnston. The Little Rabbit Who Wanted Red Wings by Elizabeth Matheson and Tiffany Janusz, The Animal, The Vegtable and John D. Jones by Alisa Burgos, Tricia Beavers and Greg Beemiller, Funnybones by Daniel Weiss, Cat in the Hat by Lynda Barney, Harold's Trip to the Sky by Steven Kurchoff, El by Mrs. Wiley, Wacky Wednesday by Crissy Brown, and Angie Charles, Pussin Boots by Tonya Burgos and Stephanie Jorgenson, M-n-M and the Haunted House by Julie Roxberg and Tiffany Long and Return of the Jedi by Michael Levas and Brent Miltner. I think everyone did a good job and I think next year will be good too! Our thanks to Mrs. Wilson and all of Erie students who participated in making the annual Book Parade a success.

Photo by Peter Ensenberger

And, when a student comes rushing excitedly into the library with a clipping in his or her hand, I know that the book parade has made the local newspaper.

The enjoyment of the parade continues following the actual event since special props, exceptional headgear, and floats are displayed in the library, and the library echoes with "Oh, look! There's . . ." for a few days. Of course, in prominent view on a table, are the titles represented in the parade, now available for circulation.

In summary, then, costumed characters may join a class or schoolwide Book Character Costume Day. During such a day, they may merely engage in normal routine while wearing their costumes; they may be introduced casually within the classroom; they may parade informally around the school; or they may be shown off at an assembly and judged.

They may also be *presented*, most frequently with planned and practiced short introductions

    1. to a single classroom;

2. in an exchange program between two or more classrooms;
3. in tours of a. the playground,
             b. the cafeteria,
             c. each classroom of the school;
4. in programs presented to the entire school, limited to library club participation or a maximum of 15–20 students;
5. in school-wide parades.

(A postscript was mandated by my excitement at reading about *another* way of using costumed book characters, one to which our young people should surely relate: a TV talk show. A brief description and a related photograph appear in Diane Monson's "Characterization in Literature: Realistic and Historic Fiction," a chapter in *Children's Literature in the Reading Program*, edited by Bernice E. Cullinan and published by the International Reading Association, 1987.)

XI. IDEAS FOR A CLASS PRESENTATION OF A SINGLE TITLE

In the previous chapter, the ways suggested for presenting book characters have mainly utilized the characters as individuals, or, at the most, in small groups. This chapter will detail how book characters may be presented in larger groups in a situation where each class works only on one title.

A librarian's choice of structuring a parade with an "assignment" of one title per class would be a good one to make in terms of the heightened feelings of pride and community that would be likely to be gained within a class. With this kind of assignment, all students may take some part in the parade, whether it is a small one, like coloring in the letters for a sign, or the larger one of portraying the main character from the title in a mini-drama.

Of course, classroom book celebrations of a single title need not be limited to parade times or National Children's Book Week productions. They may take place any time during the school year: for an all-school assembly at a flag raising, "Our class would like to share with you scenes from a book we've enjoyed," or for proud parents at a program put on in the classroom itself. The presentation could also be just part of a "fun Friday" for the students themselves, savored by teacher and students alike, after a week of particularly disciplined or difficult work.

The following flyer, however, was developed to aid classroom teachers in preparing a title for a book celebration assembly which is followed by a parade.

You are invited to join in a celebration of National Children's Book Week. The following are ideas and tips for preparing a classroom entry for the parade:

1. Choose a title you have read to the class that they have enjoyed or one that the majority of the class knows. (Check with me to make sure it does not duplicate another class's choice.)

2. As a class, brainstorm ideas for depicting this title. Call in the library staff to help with ideas. Remember, exaggeration will make your presentation vivid, memorable, and fun.

3. List the main characters.

4. For these characters think of
   a. special articles of clothing or costuming needs such as animal faces
   b. specific incidents in the plot
   c. distinctive phrases said by each of these characters
   d. items the characters possess, unique to them alone

5. Decide on whether or not to include minor characters.

6. Think about what would be appropriate as a large backdrop for the setting such as a building or an outdoor scene.

7. Decide on number, wording, and size of signs. (Remember, some of the audience will be about 60 feet away.)

Class Presentation of a Single Title

      a. title and author
      b. labels for characters or props
      c. complimentary comments about the book

8. Examining ideas developed in 4.b., decide on the focus for a mini-dramatization, not more than a minute or so in length, that would show responses typical of the characters in the story. Work on dialogue and action for this presentation.

9. Decide on the wording for the introduction of your representation of the book in addition to the wording of any microphone comments to be made during the mini-dramatization.

10. Advertise for props and costume details not available from class members.

11. Plan on using one or two art periods for construction of the background scene, headgear, paper costumes, and signs. Make all oversize to be clear at a distance.

12. Plan on using 2 or 3 language periods for the writing of the script and repeated practice of the dramatization.

13. Book a time a few days before the parade to practice lining up, the use of space for the dramatization, and the use of the microphone.

14. Have your stage participants ready to join other classes in a noncostumed "dress rehearsal" the day before the parade.

15. Turn in this entry form by _____ .

- -

Class:

Title of Book:

Characters on Stage   Students Playing these Characters

Announcer(s):

Script for Introduction (may be attached):

Summary of Dramatic Action:

Special Assistance Needs (volunteer parent helper, backdrop storage place, special music, etc.):

Since the teachers at Erie are now experienced in this kind of celebration, I have abbreviated the guide as shown below. This is the most recent edition:

A GUIDE FOR PLANNING A
PRESENTATION FOR A BOOK CELEBRATION

1. Decide on a single title to present, either one that you and your class have enjoyed together or one that at least most of the students have read on their own.

2. Brainstorm together about

    a. the main characters—their idiosyncratic dress, speech, habits or predicaments

    b. available props that suggest the character (These should be exaggerated to allow good visualization by the audience. Examples are a brick and trowel for the third little pig or a bottle of "Delayed Action Mouse-Maker Formula 86" for the boy/mouse in *The Witches*.)

    c. available costuming materials

    d. an interesting scene or brief interaction among characters (Make this short—2 minutes—and as packed with drama as the book permits.) Simple introduction of the characters is O.K., too.

    e. use of announcer and/or narrator

    f. need for any sign in addition to one for the title

3. Plan for one practice during library period the week of _____.

4. Turn in the following by _____.

- -

Class: _____

Title Planned for Presentation: _____

Type of Presentation Tentatively Planned:

Number of Students Who Will Be "On Stage:" _____

We will supply our own announcer _____

We would prefer to have a sixth grade library club member as an announcer: _____

We need the following help from the library staff:

The following grade-by-grade outline of titles that lend themselves to presentation by a classroom might be utilized as a source for ideas. For each grade, I have tried to select at least one modern and one not-so-modern piece of literature with which to work.

Class Presentation of a Single Title

Kindergarten

For kindergartners, I could see the old favorite, *Ask Mr. Bear*, by Marjorie Flack, acted out in pantomime. Danny would appear first, scratching his head. Then, in turn, he would meet the various animals in the story, with his arms outstretched, tilting his head in a questioning manner. Each time the animal would proffer its wares, Danny would shake his head, "No," moving his hands back and forth in front of the animal in a "stop" gesture, until he reached Mr. Bear. (Perhaps an older, taller child could be imported to play the part of Mr. Bear for the occasion, or, what fun, if the teacher could feel comfortable in such a role.) The other animals would huddle in fright as Mr. Bear, a frown built into his mask, would pretend to whisper into Danny's ear. Then Danny would skip merrily to greet his mother. With his hands behind his back, he would smile and nod happily about her "gift," showing anticipation on his face. I would have the mother put her finger to her forehead and then ask a question in pantomime three times, her hands stretched out and eyebrows raised. Danny would respond with vigorous shakes of his head each time. Finally, after the mother's gesture and shrug indicating "give up," Danny would give her the bear hug.

A silent pantomime might be fun for a presentation within the classroom itself. For a presentation to an audience other than the class, probably an announcer would be necessary. He or she would provide a running commentary on Danny's actions:

> "In *Ask Mr. Bear*, Danny is wondering what to get his mother for her birthday. He goes to a hen (pause for the hen to cluck out loud, perhaps, and for the pantomime to take place) but he doesn't want an egg. He meets a goose . . . but his mother already has a pillow filled with feathers. The goat . . . offers his cream for making cheese; the sheep . . . wool for a blanket; and the cow . . . some milk. But Danny's mother already has these things. The animals tell him to visit Mr. Bear. [The animals would all point in one direction and then huddle back in fear.] Mr. Bear growls a little but finally whispers a secret in Danny's ear. Danny goes back to his mother and asks her if she can guess what he has for her birthday. She tries . . . but just cannot guess. So . . . Danny gives his mother a great big . . . bear hug!"*

The narration above needs to be timed exactly right with the action. Again, an older child may be recruited for this task or the teacher may choose to narrate the dramatization. Given enough time for practice, however, some kindergartners would be able to perform more than satisfactorily in this role.

One sign, the title, would be adequate for a parade. A "Happy Birthday!" sign for the end would be nice to add. If the "play" is performed in the classroom, normal-sized props—a real egg (blown out), an empty milk carton, etc.—are fine; however; for large group viewing and parade purposes, oversized cardboard props, possibly labelled and *feather* and *egg* are preferable. A meadow scene could be made for a backdrop. It could be exchanged for a forest scene at the appearance of Mr. Bear or a few children costumed as trees could merely position themselves in front of the meadow backdrop at his entrance.

Although making three-dimensional headgear for the animals in *Ask Mr. Bear* is a relatively simple operation (see Chapter III, page 21), perhaps you might feel more comfortable for a first time experience with helping children make the stick puppet type of mask; or, for that matter, in choosing a different title to illustrate.

---

*Adapted with permission of Macmillan Publishing Company from *Ask Mr. Bear* by Marjorie Flack. Copyright 1958 by Macmillan Publishing Company; copyright renewed 1986.

In this light, costume production for *The Very Hungry Caterpillar* would be an easier task. For this story, the child could merely hold large cardboard shapes in front of himself or herself, or wear simple paper body drapes for the fruit and other edible items. The ice cream cone, for example, could be drawn and painted on bulletin board paper and sandwich-boarded over the child's head. Only one costume, that of the beautiful butterfly, would need special time and attention to make it spectacular. (See also pages 18 and 27.) The story line is again short enough for a narrator to tell it as the "characters" come on stage. "On Monday, he ate through one juicy apple. . . . On Tuesday, he ate through two . . . , etc."

This title has the advantage of being able to accommodate an entire class "on stage" rather than limiting some children to just the production end of the celebration. This being the case, perhaps the title might be better chosen for a parent or school performance rather than an all-school parade. For the latter, the size of the group might be unwieldy and there is also the need to have some children left to form an audience.

A final suggestion for kindergarten level, one that would appeal to the teacher who enjoys focusing on traditional literature that may have been missed by many of today's generation of children, is a parade entry or a program consisting of a small number of groups of Mother Goose characters. Jack and Jill, holding a pail between them, Jack with a bandaged head; Little Bo Peep with her crook and lamb in hand; and so on, as listed in Chapter IV, page 38, would all be colorful and fun.

First Grade

Although obviously my choices are arbitrary, our Erie first graders have been so tickled by the series by Harry Allard on "The Stupids" that I could not resist choosing to celebrate them for and with this grade level. Older students, however, as evidenced by their repeated return to the easy reader, *Wacky Wednesday*, would not be averse to enjoying the absolute and utter silliness of the Stupid family either.

From any of the titles one could draw a treasure of easily presentable, chuckle-producing characters and props.

Stepping out might be Stanley Q. Stupid, with his stockings on his ears. Mrs. Stupid would wear a stuffed striped cat on her head, with dignity, of course. Buster and Petunia would be accompanied by their dog wearing a sign with his name, "Kitty," in addition to the Indian feather bonnet on his head. Naturally, they all would be joined by Grandfather Stupid, complete with white beard and moustache, sailor suit, striped socks, and hula hoop.

The pictures of a butterfly, duck, dog, and glass of water with their respective labels of "cow," "bus," "fish," and "Lake Stupid" could be presented to the audience singly, between characters, or they could be mounted on a large backdrop representation of a wall.

An announcer could also introduce the numerous characters at the Stupid's ball. Here, Mrs. Stupid would be coiled in thin paper strips, resembling her spaghetti outfit. General George Washing Machine, costumed with tri-cornered hat and a body box with a circle on the front, the details of the controls on the top and an electric cord dangling from the rear included, should not be missed. Nor should the red-ringleted and moustached gentleman who would make his way across the schoolyard on skis (cardboard), in a striped nightgown with a candelabra on his head. The hen for the top of Dot's head might be a little challenging to construct but Grandfather Stupid's Easter bunny costume would not. The white beard, moustache, and pumpkin would be easy to execute. Finding someone to play Grandfather, who could do justice to the necessarily booming, "Ho, ho, ho!" would be a bit more difficult.

A suggestion for the first grade teacher with less interest in silliness and more interest in folk literature would be the choice of a class presentation of the three Billy Goats Gruff.

Class Presentation of a Single Title 113

Painting the bridge, stream and green pasture for a backdrop would make an excellent assignment for classroom artists. Somewhat of a minus, however, is the limited number of characters. Perhaps this problem could be alleviated, in part, by the addition of some children as trees for the pasture. And, of course, the bridge, the pasture, and the stream could be paper-draped children instead of a painted scene.

Goat headgear could either be the flat mask, held by a stick or applied to a box or paper sack for over the head, or a three dimensional one with a snout. In either case, the important factors are the horns, the goat beards, and some indication of the increase in size from the smallest to largest. Do not fret over goats walking on two feet. Significant effects are the headgear and the "trip-trap" sounds. The goats may do their own trip trap sound effects (differentiated for each size, please), or the bridge, if represented by a child, may contribute that essential part of the presentation.

If a classic story with a greater number of characters is desired, you might try Wanda Gag's *Millions of Cats*.

Second Grade

During my guided narrative dramatizations with primary students, I have found that second graders have done the most noteworthy job with the beloved story by Polushkin, *Mother, Mother, I Want Another*. Nevertheless, during a recent Erie parade, it was a group of fourth graders that made an excellent presentation of this title.

Polushkin's book lends itself to a quick, mini-drama treatment. Mother Mouse (Bedtime Stories conspicuously printed on a "book" tucked under her arm) would be helping baby mouse (in pajamas and perhaps holding a toothbrush) to bed. The bed may be there in actuality, but it need not be present for understandable action to take place. A "security blanket" and/or pillow clutched by baby mouse will suffice.

What *is* necessary is a penetratingly high, clear rendition by baby mouse of "Mother, mother, I want another!" preceded and followed by loud sobs.

Mother Mouse would draw forward Mrs. Duck, who would say, after a vigorous quack or two, "Don't cry, baby mouse, I'll bring you some fat wet worms." Baby mouse's repetitive cry, "Mother, mother . . ." would increase in vigor. In turn, Mrs. Frog would offer big fat flies; Mrs. Pig would offer carrots; and Mrs. Donkey, song book opened in front of her, would offer to sing a lullabye. All would be rejected noisily by baby mouse, who would then spit out, between sobs, "I want another bedtime kiss!" All animals, after exclamations of surprise, would then kiss baby mouse, in a satisfying conclusion to the problem.

Again, a microphone narrator, delineating the basic thread of the story, helps to clarify the drama to onlookers. "Mrs. Duck went to get Mrs. Frog" and so on, would be fitting comments, with a final wind-up of "And baby mouse went happily to sleep." Again, quite a bit of practice will be necessary to manage smooth timing on this effort.

Having the children playing Mother and baby mouse wear ears on their own heads and the children playing the other animals use face masks on sticks worked out well for the kissing scene. (The kissing, of course, was accompanied by loud smacks of the lips.)

For the second grade teacher wanting to delve more into folk literature, Cinderella or Snow White make popular choices.

Cinderella's cast may be expanded by the addition of a number of couples dancing at the ball. A child as a grandfather clock, bonging out the count of twelve, is a nice touch. And a shoe definitely needs to be lost at some point during the proceedings.

A depiction of Snow White calls at least for a mirror scene and an apple scene. From the point of view of most students, it also calls for Disney's individual characterization of the seven dwarfs. Although bowdlerization is somewhat intellectually offensive to me, I have found myself thoroughly enjoying Sleepy, Dopey, Grumpy, and the other dwarves who have appeared at various Erie parades.

Third Grade

Classroom choices for third grade could definitely move to fiction. *Charlie and the Chocolate Factory* and *Charlotte's Web* have been perennial third grade favorites at my school.

I would prefer, however, to stick with titles the majority of children at this grade level could read. Thus, I might choose the magnificent Aardema offering, *Why Mosquitoes Buzz in People's Ears*, for a production.

A commentary from the microphone would delineate the bare bones story as the farmer, mosquito, iguana, python, rabbit, crow, monkey, and Mother Owl make their appearances. A Sun should be in readiness off stage. Melodramatic entrances could be made. For example, the rabbit could scamper across the stage area in a flash. The crow could "Caw" raucously while flying about and the monkey would scream, "Kili wili," while jumping about hysterically.

After the entrance of a sad Mother Owl and an explanation of the ensuing problem by the narrator, King Lion would stalk in and in a loud and commanding voice cry, "Calling all animals, calling all animals!" The animals would gather around the council fire and murmur among themselves, each pointing to another. Finally iguana would be sent for and questioned by King Lion. After the general outcry, "Punish the mosquito!" followed by three hoots from the satisfied Mother Owl, allowing the Sun to come up, the storyteller can finish off with the explanatory preface to the final "KAPAO!" The repetitive accusations in the text could be skipped over for brevity's sake.

A mixture of costuming treatments does not seem to bother an elementary school audience. In this case, the lion and monkey, for example, would be fitted in attire which would allow movement of the child's body, namely headgear and "bodi-puppet" costuming. The python, however, could be an inanimate roll of material with marionette-like string and stick, operated by a student in full view of the audience.

On the classic side of the picture, I would likely choose the nursery favorite, "The Three Little Pigs."

If perhaps you are thinking that this story is too juvenile a choice, you might like to know that Erie School sixth graders did this one admirably and with great pleasure. Indeed, any grade, even ones including those sophisticates who dismiss folk tales as "for babies," will usually work willingly on such a production, with the understanding that it's "for the kindergarteners to enjoy."

For any grade, then, a mini-dramatization of the adventures of the pigs could be narrated. The narration would include the men with the hay, sticks, and bricks in addition to the main characters if you were trying to create more onstage positions. The portrayal of the frustration of the wolf at being unable to blow down the house made of bricks would make a suitable ending.

Short tubular snouts on face masks suffice for the pigs. The bundles of straw, sticks, and a few bricks must not be overlooked, but they may be created artificially, of course, if acquisition of the real thing is a problem.

The wolf character needs special attention. Headgear, showing the wolf's mouth partially open, with teeth in view and tongue protruding from the side, would be ideal. Even more important is the selection of a child who has the ability to enter into the character without embarrassment, huffing and puffing in an exaggerated manner, and finally slinking away, defeated.

Class Presentation of a Single Title

The three-sided cardboard "brick" house worn by an additional sixth grader was large enough to allow the three pigs some shelter as they peeked out at the wolf. Third graders would find the construction of a similar house easy enough to manage.

Fourth Grade

For a fourth grade presentation, my first choice would probably be their favorite, *Tales of a Fourth Grade Nothing*. For this title, a medley of scenes of memorable incidents might be attempted, as from the following:

The incident where Fudgie is pretending to be a dog: The family could be sitting and eating at a table. Fudge would be under the table, saying, "I'm a doggie. Woof . . . woof . . . woof!" The mother would ask Fudge if he would like to eat on the floor like a dog. She would hand down a plate of food in response to his nods and barks, and eventually, as he eats, she would reach down and pet his head, remarking, "Good doggie."

Alternatively, another incident related to food could be chosen. The family would be around the table as before. Fudge would demand and get cornflakes instead of the food the others would be eating. Then, as he still did not eat, father would warn, "Fudge, you will eat that cereal or you will wear it." Fudge would respond, "NO EAT . . . NO EAT. . . ." Father would dump the bowl of cornflakes over Fudgie's head.

If some structure that could represent a jungle gym is available, the episode in the park could be played. Peter, Sheila, and Jimmy could be scuffling and Sheila could be chanting, "Peter's got the cooties. Peter's got the cooties." Meanwhile, Fudgie would climb on the jungle gym, waving his arms. "Fudgie's a birdie. Fudgie's a birdie. Fly, birdie . . . fly." He would proceed to fall on his face.

If smaller children were in good supply, Peter could lead the birthday party participants in dancing with balloons to music, looking self-conscious, of course. As typical, Ralph could be eating while dancing, Jennie might be trying to bite the balloon, and Sam would be whimpering on the fringe of the activity. Fudge, now with two blacked-out front teeth, would be holding and glaring at the book that was his birthday gift. A commentator to introduce each child might be included.

If procuring a duplicate of a Toddle-Bike is not a problem, the events that took place at Mr. Hatcher's place of employment could be re-enacted. Fudge, tricked by Peter and the adults and bribed with Oreo cookies, would ride the bike for the filming of the commercial.

Without any doubt, the scene that preceded Fudge's trip to the hospital should be represented. A sign might read, "Friday, May 10." Peter would appear, carrying an empty turtle bowl. (Perhaps the bowl could be labelled with Dribble's name.) Fudge would be smiling and giggling over Peter's repeated and frantic, "Where's Dribble!! What did you do with my turtle?!" Dialogue between Mrs. Hatcher and Fudgie would follow, ending with Fudge's statement, "All gone turtle. Down Fudgie's tummy." Mother would make a panicky telephone call and Fudgie would be carried off on a stretcher by two men in white. He would wave engagingly at the audience. The scene could end with Peter, walking a dog. He would announce, "This is my new dog. His name is Turtle."

Costumes would be simple everyday clothing. A horizontally striped T-shirt would be a good choice for Fudgie.

More characters and more costume-making would be necessary for a presentation of E. B. White's *Charlotte's Web*, another fourth grade "best book." Small interactions between characters as they are introduced would hold audience interest.

The commentator would introduce Mr. and Mrs. Arable and their daughter Fern. Fern would start pleading with her father to spare the pig's life. (Mr. Arable would have an ax in his hand.)

Mr. Zuckerman would be announced and would appear with his pail of slops. He would tap the pail and call, "Come pig! Come pig!" and Wilbur would enter.

Wilbur would follow the pail on stage and then sit down and say, "I'm lonely." A voice off stage would say, "Salutations!" and Charlotte would walk in. The two might engage in a little dialogue. Then Wilbur might exclaim, "Oh Charlotte, it's nice to have a friend but . . . I don't want to die." He would cry. Charlotte would state, "I'm going to save you." In response to Wilbur's "How?" she would say, "That remains to be seen." Wilbur would move off stage, sniffling.

Meanwhile Charlotte would pretend to be working on something in her hands. On Wilbur's return, paper letters saying, "Some pig!" held by Charlotte above Wilbur's head could be admired and exclaimed over by the rest of the cast.

A final announcement might be, "And keeping Wilbur company now are . . . Charlotte's children!" Three tiny spiders would enter and encircle Wilbur.

Incidentally, the chase scene with Wilbur running between Lurvy's legs could be included to add more drama. However, it also would be more difficult to stage than the above.

Props would include an ax for Mr. Arable and at least one bucket for Mr. Zuckerman. Any animals included, other than Charlotte and her children (see page 16 for costuming for Charlotte), might be best done with face masks, either attached or unattached. I would like to see two masks made for Wilbur: one showing a worried downcast expression and one showing radiant happiness. The exit planned for when Charlotte fumbles with her letters prior to producing the "Some pig!" would allow time for the changeover off stage.

Fifth Grade

Although I know that *Charlie and the Chocolate Factory* is one of the offerings of Hollywood and although I know that this title has been spoken of with less than acclaim by people with lofty literary tastes, I still would make it one of my choices for a fifth grade production. I tend to be swayed by student enthusiasm.

Again, short introductions as a narrator spins the story thread would be quite an acceptable treatment. Four students, dressed in nightwear and representing the grandparents, would hobble slowly across the stage. Mr. Bucket would appear, screwing the cap on the top of an oversize tube of toothpaste. Mrs. Bucket, holding a stock pot labelled "cabbage soup," might pause to ladle some out to the grandparents.

Then would come Charlie, scarf over head, dragging school books in a strap in his hand, wearing ragged clothing, and carrying his birthday present—an oversized version of Wonka's Whipple-Scrumptious fudgemallow Delight. All on stage would show extreme disappointment when Charlie unwraps the bar and it is evident that there is not a Golden Ticket inside.

The stage would clear and Charlie, who would be walking slowly and painfully, rubbing his stomach to indicate hunger, would discover the dollar bill.

The storekeeper and Charlie would be very excited over the appearance of the Golden Ticket on the purchase of his second candy bar. Rushing home, Charlie would be joined by the rest of his family and he and Grandpa Joe would hold hands and spin around with delight.

The narrator would say, "So, the next day . . . Charlie met Mr. Wonka . . . and here he is!!" Mr. Wonka would be dressed in black top hat, plum tailcoat, green trousers, and gray gloves, and be equipped with a black goatee and a gold-topped walking cane. He would express pleasure at the children coming on the tour of the factory and perform a little dance.

Class Presentation of a Single Title

Introductions of the four other children would follow:

Augustus Gloop would be fattened by pillows and be eating non-stop.

Veruca Salt, in "silver mink coat," would be having a temper tantrum about wanting a squirrel.

Violet Beauregarde would be colored purple (1 tablespoon soft shortening, 2 tablespoons corn starch, 2 drops red food coloring, 1 drop blue food coloring) and would be chewing gum vigorously.

Mike Teavee, wearing a windbreaker decorated with a picture of the Lone Ranger as well as many belts from which guns would be hanging, would be leaping into the air and firing one or another of the guns.

The Oompa-Loompas, the smallest children in the class, or imports from a lower grade level, could do shortened chants between the introductions of each of the above characters, summing up their fate. (The school music teacher might help in developing and perfecting the unison chant.) Finally, a genial Mr. Wonka would shake hands with Charlie and congratulate him on earning ownership of the factory.

The deerskin and leaf costumes for the Oompa-Loompas would be the most challenging part of the preparations for staging this title. Tunics of bulletin board paper would do the job nicely, however. Perhaps shopping bag paper, crumpled before construction of the garment to enhance the leather look, could be used for the male Oompa-Loompas. An authentic look would be captured by covering only one shoulder and by making the lower edge of the material jagged. Green tunics for the females might have additional separate leaf shapes placed over the bodice and the skirt.

Garbage could be thrown over Veruca in the middle of her temper tantrum, and a quick exchange of a doll for Mike Teavee might be made during the fourth chant by the Oompa-Loompas. The interior of a factory showing many intriguing doors or an elevator in the sky could be sketched for a back drop and would be nice but not essential.

Incidentally, for the time constraints of an all-school celebration, Tony Fanucci's fifth graders simply had Mr. Wonka greet each winner and Grandpa Joe outside the factory, as in Chapter XIV, "Mr. Willy Wonka." Each had a momentary interaction with Mr. Wonka, in character, and the scene ended with everyone following him, "Through the big red door, please!" offstage. For a longer production, see footnote on page 124.

A second title appropriate for fifth grade might be Madeleine L'Engle's Newbery-winner, *A Wrinkle in Time*. In actuality, it was a fourth grade that chose to present this title at an Erie celebration. Student teacher Ann Wood, with students brainstorming all the positive concepts utilized to fight the Dark Thing, developed a news-reporting script as a vehicle to include all the characters *and*, happily, the entire class on stage. The following is an adaptation of their script:

Announcer: *A Wrinkle in Time* by Madeleine L'Engle was the book Mrs. Schaab's class chose for today's celebration. And right now, entering studio KXYZ-TV are the characters from *A Wrinkle in Time!*

Reporter: Good morning, ladies and gentlemen. This is Chad Roggentein of KXYZ-TV bringing you the interstellar news live from the earth. We have received reports of a Dark Thing at large in the universe, an evil cloud that spreads hate and negativity wherever it goes.

[Camazotz children march across stage in a "gliding mechanical" manner.]

Reporter: Who are you?!—An Army?

Camazotz Children [unison monotone]: No, we're children. We're from Camazotz. We're just going for a walk.

Mrs. Whatsit: They're from a planet that has given in to the Black Thing. On Camazotz, everyone looks just alike and acts just alike.

Reporter: And who, madam, are you?

Mrs. Whatsit: I'm Mrs. Whatsit. These are my friends, Mrs. Which, Mrs. Who, and Aunt Beast.

Mrs. Who: And this is The Happy Medium.

Happy Medium: We will never give up fighting the Dark Thing and we think that there are others fighting with us.

Reporter: Many planets have already given in, according to reports received here at KXYZ.

Mrs. Which: That is true. And sadly, there are many planets still in danger of giving in to the Black Thing.

Reporter: Some earth people who have survived contact with the Black Thing are here to talk about what it was like.

Mr. Murry: We're the Murry family and this is our friend Calvin.

Calvin: [Waves at camera]

[Lights go out!]

Reporter: What happened?!!

Charles Wallace: It's the Black Thing! The forces of darkness are trying to take over the earth. We must fight! *I* still believe in love! And in happiness! And in personal achievement!

Mr. Murry: I believe in intelligence. And in fighting for what you believe in!

Meg: I believe in freedom! I believe in sharing!

Calvin: I believe in helping and I believe in peace!

Mr. Murry: I believe in togetherness! I believe in truth!

Sandy: I believe in courage! And in sensitivity!

Dennys: I believe in trusting yourself! I believe in giving!

Aunt Beast: The people of earth believe in beauty! They believe in caring!

Mrs. Who: Earth still believes in courtesy! And in confidence!

Mrs. Which: The people of earth believe in faith and in not giving up!

Mrs. Whatsit: The earth still believes in optimism! People here believe in excellence!

[Lights go on]

Reporter: The Black Thing is gone! (Everyone cheers.) KXYZ News is happy to report that, at this point in time, the earth shows *no signs at all* of giving in to the Black Thing! This has been your up-to-the-minute news report from KXYZ. Thank you and have a good day.

The reporter and the Murry family spoke from one microphone, the non-earthlings from another. The reporter wore a hat with a PRESS label tucked in its band. Ties were appropriate attire for most of the males. Red hair would have been ideal for Mrs. Murry. Meg needed eyeglasses, as did Mrs. Who, large glittering ones for the latter. The Camazotz children were in identical loose jerkins garnered from the PE department. Mrs. Whatsit was costumed as the dumpy lady in a long overcoat swathed in multicolored scarves and shawls rather than as the handsome white winged creature of Uriel. Mrs. Which wore a black robe, witch's hat, and carried a broomstick. The Happy Medium donned a long dress and turban

Class Presentation of a Single Title

and held her crystal ball. Putting a nylon stocking over tall Aunt Beast's face and attaching soft gray yarn "tentacles" for ears and hair conveyed her characteristics: a blanket over the shoulders avoided the necessity of creating four arms.

Although students were forewarned on morning announcements about the planned "lights out," the complete darkness did unnerve the mixed-age audience. Opening the auditorium door a crack solved the problem.

In favor of clear communication, no attempt was made to duplicate Mrs. Which's unique form of speech.

I seem to have selected two fantasies for fifth grade, oblivious to fifth graders' very positive response to realistic fiction. Considering this omission, I might suggest a production of *How to Eat Fried Worms*. Such a presentation would please both the class and the audience, save for a few squeamish souls.

On first examination of this title, I was disappointed by the fact that the main characters number only four. On further perusal, however, I could see ways of involving more characters. The use of episodes, such as the one where Billy's mother presents the Whizbang Worm Delight at the family table or the one in which the boys' use of the siren rouses an entire neighborhood would bring more students into the action. See page 71 for ideas for props. (Thomas Rockwell, the author himself, has written a dramatization of the entire action of this title in *How to Eat Fried Worms and Other Plays*, published by Delacorte.)

Sixth Grade

Sixth graders would likely enjoy presenting the action in "Miss Boland's Victrola," from *Soup and Me*. Even the *idea* of the large nurse showing the class dance steps using a chair as a partner is hilarious.

I could see four scenes:

1. A demonstration of a dance step by uniformed Nurse Boland to music from her victrola for Miss Kelly's class. (A decision must be made about whether or not to include her pratfall.) Identifiable characters would have to include Soup, Rob, Norma Jean Bissell, and Janice Riker. Perhaps two more anonymous pairs would round off the class.

2. Name-drawing from a can held by Miss Boland to determine which girls would be each boy's partner. Obvious disgust would be shown by Soup at the time of the drawing and later during the third scene.

3. The practice of particular dance steps by the couples. Miss Kelly would be keeping time with her ruler; Miss Boland would still be dancing with her chair. Soup would keep as far away from Janice as possible and still dance and he would look sorrowful. Janice would lead vigorously and stomp on Soup's toe if he got out of line or out of step.

4. The Spring Dance itself. Rob would carry in a punch bowl, hear news about Norma Jean Bissell's chicken pox, and see Soup arrive on crutches. He would be ordered by Miss Kelly to dance with Janice Riker.

A scene from the same title, equally satisfying to the audience, would be a representation of the chapter, "Janice Riker Strikes Again." See page 15 for a description of Erie School's effort at this one.

A more serious title for sixth grade presentation would be Lloyd Alexander's *The Black Cauldron*. One scene would be more than enough to work on for this title. Avoiding scenes with violence, I would choose to illustrate the happenings in the chapter entitled "The Price."

Some introductory detailing of the importance of the retrieval or destruction of the Black Cauldron would be necessary in preface to the action. Then, Fflewddur and Eilonwy, hanging onto the rings, Gurgi, the side, and Taran, the handle of the Black Crochan, would move onstage, They would be struggling, sobbing, and twisting with their efforts to tear their hands loose from the pot.

Ooddu, Orwen, and Orgoch, in flapping night robes and crone visages, would enter and a shortened version of the verbal interactions in the chapter itself would precede the freeing of the four from the cauldron.

The crones would ask a price for the cauldron. Taran's offer of his sword and of his horse; Gurgi's, of his wallet that magically provides food on request; Eilonwy's, of first, the ring given to her by Prince Gwydion, and then, the golden sphere; and finally, Fflewddur's offer of his harp would be all rejected. Eventually, Taran, calling to the crones as they leave, would proffer the brooch, the gift of Adaon, son of Taliesin, and valuable to the wearer as a source for knowledge, truth, and love. The crones would accept this offer.

The scene could close with the four using iron bars and hammers in a futile attempt to destroy the cauldron. A cackling laugh and an explanation from Ooddu of the only way to destroy the cauldron would be the final note, as the four freeze in horror at a distance from it.

Historical costume books would have to be consulted for pictures of appropriate clothing for the Arthurian-flavored time period. A backdrop of the grey marshes of Morva with the low sod and branch covered cottage at the side of a mound would be nice to add.

Finally, a third title for a sixth grade presentation, one popular with presenters and audience alike, is Bill Brittain's *The Wish Giver*. At a recent celebration of books at Erie School, the following mini-dramatization of this title, written by sixth grader Renee Smith and her classmates in the gifted program, was performed. (Adapted in this format for classroom presentation from *The Wish Giver* by Bill Brittain. Copyright © 1983 by William Brittain. Reprinted by permission of Harper & Row, Publishers, Inc.)

> **Narrator:** We are portraying the story of *The Wish Giver* by Bill Brittain. The wish giver is Thaddeus Blinn who grants a wish to each of four people: Polly Kemp, Rowena Jervis, Adam Fiske, and Stew Meat, the owner of the local store.
>
> **The Wish Giver:** I will grant you each one wish for 50¢, but make your choice of words with care. [Hands out cards.]
>
> **Narrator:** Polly Kemp, a bratty child who wants to be popular, makes her wish. . . .
>
> **Polly Kemp:** I wish everyone would like me, Agatha and Eunice especially.
>
> **Agatha & Eunice:** Polly Kemp, you're downright dumb!!
>
> **Polly:** Why, you stupid! . . . ignorant! . . . JUG-A-RUM! JUG-A-RUM! [Claps both hands over mouth.]
>
> **Leland & Lenora:** She couldn't say anything bad or she would go JUG-A-RUM like a bullfrog.
>
> **Narrator:** Rowena Jervis, a teenager in love with the salesman, Henry Piper, makes her wish.
>
> **Rowena:** I wish Henry Piper would set down roots and stay forever.
>
> **Sam Waxman:** He *did* set down roots. He turned into a tree!
>
> **Henry:** Rowena Jervis! How could you do such a thing?! Get me out of this mess right now!! [Clutches a paper tree with both hands, his head framed by a hole in the trunk.]
>
> **Narrator:** Adam Fiske, whose family lacks water on their farm, makes his wish.

Uncle Poot: [Dowser rod in hand.] There's no water under *this* farm.

Adam: I wish we had water all over this farm.

Mother: It's raining!

Father: Water is shooting up all over the farm!

[All wishers run to Stew Meat.]

Stew Meat: Polly, Adam, Rowena!! What are you doing here? I've already locked up.

Kids Together: Have you used your wish yet?

Stew: No, why?

All Kids: Wish for me! Wish for me!

Stew: Wait!! I know what to wish for! I wish that all three of these young'uns will have their wishes canceled out this very minute.

[Cheers from everyone. Tree and water props are dropped to the floor.]

Three sets were on stage at the same time: a swingset/playground backdrop for Polly; a large tree, unfurled after Rowena made her wish; and a farmhouse backdrop for Adam, with rolls of blue bulletin board paper in readiness to represent the water that appeared after his wish. (Costuming included a bowler, vest, and moustache for Thaddeus Blinn, a suit for Henry Piper, a storekeeper apron for Stew Meat, frilly feminine clothing for Agatha, Eunice, and Rowena, and clothing typical of everyday wear in a farming community for the other characters. Each wisher was given a white card centered with a red spot.)

Additional Titles

Obviously, the preceding demarcation of titles by grade level is arbitrary. Just how arbitrary was very recently made evident to me when a talented group of sixth graders spontaneously put together a dramatization of *The Stupids Die* for the sixth grade end-of-the-year library periods. While viewing their enjoyment, I had a somewhat disconcerting memory of my suggestion, in this chapter, of the Stupids for first grade.

Actually, the titles and the suggested details of the above presentations have been enumerated only to serve you, possibly as models for use, but, more felicitously, as examples to initiate your thinking about titles and possible methods of treatment for presentation purposes by your own class. With your guidance, the production of ideas by a class will be impressive.

Parenthetically, for those readers who would like to start with the security of a ready-made, book-related script, a few may be found under the Drama heading of the card catalog, a few more under the heading Puppets and Puppet Plays. Some specific sources will include Champlin and Renfro's *Storytelling with Puppets* (ALA), Caroline Feller Bauer's *Presenting Reader's Theater: Plays and Poems to Read Aloud* (H. W. Wilson), and Readers Theatre Script Service (P.O. Box 178333, San Diego, CA 92117). The limitation of a class's book celebration choice to just what is available in this format is the disadvantage of this approach, however.

I have confidence that, with enough thought and planning, *any* title enjoyed as a read aloud by a class could be vividly represented for an audience. Indeed, the bringing into view of something loved by a class through creative team effort will provide a very enthusiastic "commercial" that will not be lost on onlookers.

The following titles seem to lend themselves to portrayal by a class. However, I hope that you will not limit yourself and your class to these. Actually, *any* of the large number of cumulative tales would be ideal to utilize for primary students. And again, the primary/intermediate designation is arbitrary and your choice as to grade level may well differ from mine.

Primary Titles

AUTHOR	TITLE	PAGE REFERENCES
Aardema	*Bringing the Rain to Kapiti Plain*	Kapit 62
Aardema	*Who's in Rabbit's House*	12
Aardema	*Why Mosquitoes Buzz in People's Ears*	114
Allard	*Miss Nelson Is Missing* (chosen by Erie 5th graders)	Miss Viola Swamp 64
Allard	various titles about the Stupids	12 & 112
Asch	*Popcorn*	Sam 66
Barrett	*Cloudy with a Chance of Meatballs*	Nameless characters 65
Barry	*Mr. Willowby's Christmas Tree*	65
Berenstain	*Bears in the Night*	54
———	*The Bremen Town Musicians*	42
Bonsall	*The Case of the Hungry Stranger*	Wizard 68
Bright	*Georgie and the Robbers*	6 and 9
Brown	*The Bionic Bunny Show*	13
Burningham	*Mr. Gumpy's Outing*	65
Carle	*The Very Hungry Caterpillar*	18 and 68
———	*Cinderella*	42 and 113
Cleary	*Beezus and Ramona*	71
De Paola	*Strega Nona*	Big Anthony 54
Domanska	*The Great Big Enormous Turnip*	
Eastman	*Are You My Mother?*	146
Embry	*The Blue-Nosed Witch*	12
Ets	*Play with Me*	38
Flack	*Ask Mr. Bear*	111
Freeman	*The Chalk Box*	Chalks 56
Gackenbach	*More from Hound and Bear*	Hound 62
Gag	*Millions of Cats*	113
———	*The Gingerbread Man*	44
Hogrogian	*One Fine Day*	Fox 59
Hughes	*Alfie Gets in First*	Alfie 48
Hutchins	*Goodnight Owl*	

Class Presentation of a Single Title

AUTHOR	TITLE	PAGE REFERENCES
———	*I Know an Old Lady Who Swallowed a Fly*	66
———	*Jack and the Beanstalk*	44
Janice	*Little Bear Marches in the St. Patrick's Day Parade*	63
Kalan	*Jump, Frog, Jump*	59
LaFontaine	*The North Wind and the Sun*	47
———	*The Little Red Hen*	45
McGovern	*Too Much Noise*	
Margolis	*Big Bear to the Rescue*	55
Marshall	*George and Martha* (multiple scenes)	60
Minarik	*A Kiss for Little Bear*	63
Mooser	*The Ghost with the Halloween Hiccups*	10
Mosel	*The Funny Little Woman*	60
———	*Mother Goose*	Chapter IV, 38
Noble	*The King's Tea*	
Polushkin	*Mother, Mother, I Want Another* (chosen by Erie 4th graders)	53 & 113
Rey	*Curious George Goes to the Hospital* (chosen by Erie 6th graders)	51 and 58
Sendak	*Where the Wild Things Are*	Max 64
Slobodkina	*Caps for Sale*	pedlar 20, 25, 66
———	*Snow White* (happily enacted by 6th graders)	46 and 113
———	*Three Billy Goats Gruff*	46 and 112
———	*Three Little Pigs* (again a 6th grader choice)	19, 46, 114
Tresselt	*The Mitten*	my grandfather 61
Viorst	*Alexander and the Terrible, Horrible, No Good, Very Bad Day*	48
Williams	*The Little Old Lady Who Was Not afraid of Anything*	64

Intermediate Titles

AUTHOR	TITLE	PAGE REFERENCES
Alexander	*The Black Cauldron* (the scene from "The Price")	120
Atwater	*Mr. Popper's Penguins*	27 and 78
Barrett	*Cloudy with a Chance of Meatballs*	Nameless characters 65
Baum	*The Wizard of Oz*	Dorothy 73
Bishop	*The Five Chinese Brothers*	56

AUTHOR	TITLE	PAGE REFERENCES
Blume	*Superfudge*	9
Blume	*Tales of a Fourth Grade Nothing*	75 and 115
Brittain	*The Wish Giver*	120
Byars	*The Cybil War*	73
Cleary	*Henry Huggins*	7 and 69
Dahl	*Charlie and the Chocolate Factory**	73 and 116
Dahl	*James and the Giant Peach**	75
Drury	*Champion of Merrimack County*	O Crispin 79
Gackenbach	*More from Hound and Bear*	Hound 62
Gannett	*My Father's Dragon*	Elmer 74
Hinton	*The Outsiders*	Pony Boy 81
Howe	*Bunnicula*	72
———	*I Know an Old Lady*	66
Lewis	*The Lion, the Witch, and the Wardrobe*	Aslan 70
Marshall	*George and Martha* (multiple scenes)	60
Merrill	*The Pushcart War*	Frank the Flower 74
Miles	*The Secret Life of the Underwear Champion*	Larry 77
Peck	*Soup and Me*	15, 82, & 119
Rawls	*Summer of the Monkeys*	Jay 76
Rockwell	*How to Eat Fried Worms*	71 and 119
Selden	*The Cricket in Times Square*	Chester 73
Seuss	*The Grinch Who Stole Christmas*	
Seuss	*Horton Hears a Who*	62
———	*Stone Soup*	
White	*Charlotte's Web*	16 and 115
Van Allsburg	*Jumanji*	Peter and Judy 80

See Appendix D, page 145, for sample programs for a school-wide celebration of books, for which each class presented a single title.

---

*Book length plays for both *Charlie and the Chocolate Factory* and *James and the Giant Peach* have been adapted by Richard R. George and published by Penguin.

APPENDIX A: TEACHER AND PARENT INFORMATION FORMS

1. School to Parent Flyer Regarding Book Character Costume Day

ERIE SCHOOL BOOK CHARACTER COSTUME DAY—FRIDAY, NOVEMBER 18.

EVERYONE IS INVITED TO DRESS AS A *BOOK* CHARACTER.

INTRODUCTIONS WILL BE MADE AT THE MORNING ASSEMBLY IN THE COURTYARD.

2. Librarian to Teacher Flyers

a. Regarding Pop-In Tour

11-12-73

MEANDERINGS FROM MARY:

This week is National Children's Book Week.

Caldecott and Newbery award books will be featured in the library.

Informal collection of votes for "my favorite book" will be done by having a voting box available in the library. Release of the "top ten" for Sierra Vista will be made next week.

About 35 talking book characters and book jackets will visit classrooms at intervals during the time period from 2:00–2:45 on Friday, November 16, if all goes well.

Your class will automatically be included on our itinerary if you wish us to visit. However, if you would prefer that your class not be interrupted by these visits, I certainly understand. Would you mind letting me know only if you do *NOT* want to be visited? Your name signed on this sheet of paper and placed in my box will be sufficient notice.

Thanks.

Appendixes

b. Regarding Book Character Class Exchange

10-23-79

TO: The wonderful teachers who signed up for the Erie School Book Character Class Exchange Program

FROM: Mary, the Mad Media Mistress

RE: Details of the exchange

DAY: October 31

TIMES: To be arranged between the teachers of the following paired classes.

CLASSES EXCHANGING: Ruth with John; Edna with Joanne; Georgi with Nancy; Kay with Betty; Chris with Peggy

You might want to emphasize the following to the children:

1. Choose a character from our *library* books - Mother Goose rhymes, fairy tales, and picture story books make the most distinctive characters. The exchange is in celebration of National Children's Book Week and so book characters are preferable to movie and cartoon characters.

2. *Carry the book* with you to show during the exchange.

3. Plan on *introducing yourself*. (This takes practice for best volume and delivery.) "Hi! I'm Little Rabbit from the book *Little Rabbit's Loose Tooth*. See my loose tooth wiggle?"

4. Keep costumes *simple* to put on. Paper plate or paper bag masks might work well. An article to carry representing the character is nice (e.g., the third little pig could carry a brick.) Try to think up your *own ideas*. Avoid "store costumes." (Could part of an art period be devoted to creating?)

5. Bring your costume to school *in a sack* to put on later in the day.

   NOTE: I have a reserve shelf of books with costume-making ideas in the library. They may be used in the library or checked out overnight.

   SPECIAL REQUEST:

   Sometime in the mad scramble could your class decide on five (5) children wearing book character costumes that would "make a good picture" and have them come to the library for me to take their pictures after the exchange? . . . I will be available late morning and all afternoon. I would like to avoid turning this into a "who-has-the-best-costume contest" but I think children could evaluate and vote for the most photogenic costumes in the class so the rest of the school could enjoy them too.

   HAVE A FUN TIME!! I could probably get some library mothers to help with pinning, tying, etc. . . . so call for help and we'll make up a time schedule.

c. *Regarding Book Character Class Exchange*

10/27/80

TO: Teachers who signed up for the Book Character Costume Exchange

FROM: Mary, the Mad Media Mistress

RE: Further details of the exchange and a repeat of last year's suggestions for new participants

    Day: October 31 (This Friday)

    Time: To be arranged between the following pairs of teachers

    Classes Exchanging: Ruth with John; Kay with Tony; CeCe with Peggy; Nancy with Joanne; Chris with Sandy

    Carousel with Slides of Previous Years' Costumes: This is set up and ready to go any time you want it.

You might want to emphasize the following to your children:

1. Choose a character from our *library* books. Mother Goose rhymes, fairy tales, and picture story books yield the most distinctive characters. Since the exchange is in partial celebration of National Children's Book Week, book characters are preferable to movie and cartoon characters.

2. Carry the book with you to show during the exchange. (John and Ruth found it more fun to hide the book and have the class guess the child's identity, and this sounds great.)

3. Plan on introducing yourself. (This takes practice for best volume and delivery.) "Hi! I'm Charles the crocodile from *Keep Your Mouth Closed Dear* and this is the zipper my mother put on my mouth."

4. Keep costumes simple to put on. Paper plate or paper bag masks work well. An article to carry representing the character is nice (e.g. Sam-I-Am could carry a plate with a couple of green eggs on it.) Try to think up your own ideas. Avoid store costumes and masks. (Could art period be held early this week and be devoted to creating?)

5. If possible, bring your costume to school in a sack to be put on later in the day.

The exchange is designed for fun and creative thinking and is not a competition. However, so the rest of the school will be able to enjoy the costumes (without the financial burden of taking a possible 300 slides), could your class decide on the five costumes that would "make the best picture"? Would you send these students over to the library somewhere in the mad scramble? The best times for me are from 12–1 and 2–3 but if these times are inconvenient send the children anytime and I will get the pictures. THANK YOU!

Teacher Name _____

I need _____ achievement awards for my student participants in the Book Character Costume Exchange.

Appendixes

3. Teacher to Parent Forms Regarding Book Character Class Exchange

Book Character Costume Exchange

on Halloween

in celebration of

National Children's Book Week

Sam-I-Am of Green Eggs and Ham

CHILDREN ARE TO SELECT A FAVORITE *BOOK* CHARACTER, RATHER THAN MOVIE OR CARTOON CHARACTER, TO BE. THE CHARACTER MAY BE FROM A BOOK AT HOME OR FROM SCHOOL, BUT CHILDREN SHOULD HAVE THEIR BOOK TO SHOW ALONG WITH THEIR COSTUMES. OUTFITS SHOULD BE SIMPLE TO PUT ON. PAPER BAGS OR PAPER PLATES MAY BE USED TO MAKE A MASK, IF NECESSARY. CHILDREN HAVE BEEN THINKING ABOUT THINGS THEY CAN CARRY TO HELP SHOW THEIR CHARACTER. CHILDREN ARE TO BRING COSTUMES IN A SACK TO PUT ON IN THE AFTERNOON.

Illustration reprinted by permission of Random House, Inc. from *Green Eggs and Ham* by Dr. Seuss, title page, copyright © 1960 by Dr. Seuss.

ERIE SCHOOL BOOK CHARACTER EXCHANGE

The exchange is in celebration of *National Children's Book Week*. So book characters are preferable to movie and cartoon characters.

The exchange will be on Halloween.

1. Choose a character from a library book: Mother Goose rhymes, fairy tales and picture books make the most distinctive characters.

2. *Carry the book* with you to show during the exchange.

3. *PRACTICE* introducing yourself. ("Hi! I'm Little Rabbit from the book *Little Rabbit's Loose Tooth*. See my loose tooth wiggle?")

4. Keep costumes *simple* to put on. Paper plate or paper bag masks might work well. An article to carry representing the character is nice (the 3rd little pig could carry a brick).

5. Bring your costume to school *in a sack* to put on later in the day.

APPENDIX B: PARADE SIGN-UP FORMS

1. Form for Indicating Class Interest and Suggestions

_____
Class (Teacher's Name)

_____
Student Council Rep

_____
Library Rep

1. Our class voted ☐ Yes / ☐ No on participating in a parade to help celebrate National Children's Book Week on November 19.

2. We would like the parade

   ☐ a. to be limited to book characters

   ☐ b. to include floats as well as book characters

3. Other suggestions we have about the parade are . . . (You may write on back.)

2. Class Entry Forms

It's a Parade!!

WHEN: Friday morning, November 21

WHERE: Erie School

WHAT: A celebration of National Book Week

THEME: HOORAY FOR BOOKS!

    Get those creative ideas on wheels or on foot. . . .
Represent your favorite books with floats accompanied by book characters, book characters alone, walking book jackets, and/or ten-second dramatizations.

PARADE ENTRY RULES:

1. Each participating *class* will decide on the books they would like to represent and which students will walk in the parade. (Each class is limited to representing a maximum of 3 books, using a maximum of ⅓ of the class to walk in the parade.)

2. Each participating class will fill in the entry blank below and turn it in to Mrs. Wilson in the library on or before November 14.

3. Participants in the parade will attend a walk-through rehearsal on the morning of November 20. (Floats and costumes may be kept a surprise.)

4. Each class will decide on one spokesman to introduce the class parade entries to the rest of the school on the microphone. (Signs identifying floats, etc. should be used where possible in addition to the introduction.)

- -

ERIE SCHOOL PARADE ENTRY FORM   Date _____

Teacher's Class _____

Description of entry or entries:

A. TYPE OF REPRESENTATION (Float, characters, jackets, etc.)   B. BOOK OR STORY REPRESENTED

1. _____   _____

2. _____   _____

3. _____   _____

2. Class Entry Forms (cont.)

OUR ENTRY SHEET FOR THE PARADE

for the celebration of National Children's Book Week

November 19, 1982

Teacher Name   Library Rep

                                                Student Council Rep

Rules:

1. Entries should represent characters or scenes from picture books, fiction, or biography.

2. The *maximum* number of books represented by a class may be *six* (6). However, several students may be representing each book.

3. Entries may be floats accompanied by book characters, book characters alone, walking book jackets, and/or 5-second dramatizations.

4. All entires should include either the book or a sign stating either the book title and author or (in the case of Mother Goose portrayals) the name of the character & the rhyme.

5. All participants must follow directions given by their "reps" on the day of the parade.

Book Represented	*Type of Entry*	*Students Participating*
1.		

2. Class Entry Forms (cont.)

IT'S A PARADE!!

WHEN: Friday, November 18, about 1:00 p.m.

WHERE: Erie School patio

WHAT: A celebration of National Children's Book Week

THEME: Hooray for books!

Get those creative ideas on wheels or on foot. . . . Represent your favorite books with floats accompanied by book characters, book characters alone, and/or 10 second dramatizations - or any other ways of representing books you can dream up!

Rules for Participants:

1. Each class may represent a maximum of 4 books, using a maximum of ⅓ of the class actually walking or riding in the parade.

2. The title of the book should be prominently displayed or the book itself may be carried-displayed.

3. Parade plans should be turned in to the library by 3:00 p.m. Thurs. November 10 if possible. Adjustments may be made until Tuesday, November 14. RSVP "Regrets" by Thursday, too, please.

_____ (Teacher Name)

	Book Represented	Type of Entry	Students who will be in the parade
1.			
2.			
3.			

Appendixes

3. Individual Parade Entry Form

NAME _____ ROOM #_____

For the 1984 Book Week parade I plan

on being _____

from the book _____

With me will be

    _____ as

    _____ as

    _____ as

    _____ as

I would like to be introduced ☐

I would like to speak or act something on my own instead ☐

(Please turn this form in to Mrs. Wilson or Mrs. Murphy by Monday, November 5.)

APPENDIX C: SCRIPTS

1. Script for Introduction of Playground Touring Characters

Since this week is National Library Week, members of Storytellers' Club have been out in the playground before school dressed up as a variety of "Library Loveables."

I thought this flag-raising assembly might be a good time to introduce them and let you see them all together and see if your guesses about them were correct.

Someone has been searching for her sheep this week. I think it was . . . LITTLE BO PEEP (student steps out of library door) . . . played by Wendy Kearns.

Some students thought my black and white friend was a cat, but others looked closely and saw his scrubbing brush and knew it was . . . HARRY THE DIRTY DOG . . . played by Shelli Lyon.

A pair of book characters is next. You might call one a rather interesting pest. Closely following him, probably trying to get him to take the spot off her mother's dress is the little girl whose house he visits. Margo Moss and Jamie Smith represent . . . you guessed it . . . the CAT IN THE HAT and SALLY.

A rather lumpy gentleman was waddling around the playground this week. Not only does he resemble the fattest man in the world but he has also been eating goldfish and trying to gain the world's record in goldfish swallowing. Representing THE GUINNESS BOOK OF WORLD RECORDS is John David Thompson.

The next character is a supercalifragilistic friend. She floated in and said, "Spit spot" and told me to clean up the library. Shelli Lyon played this library lovable during the week but Mrs. Gray, the sponsor of the Storytellers' Club is representing her today . . . MARY POPPINS.

Close your eyes now and say, "I believe" and then you'll be able to see the beautiful person behind the door. And do admire those lovely wings on Tiffany Rish who represents Peter Pan's friend . . . TINKER BELL.

The last library lovable looks a little mixed up. She *is* a lovable friend, but, oh, the mistakes she makes! She's the one who picks up second base and holds it so no one will steal it. I think right now she is drawing the drapes on a sketch pad. She didn't know that drawing the drapes meant pulling them shut. She means well, though, so let's make her feel good (and thank Delphina Navarette for playing her) by clapping for . . . AMELIA BEDELIA.

Appendixes

That's our last library lovable but I think it's nice to share happy things. And Storytellers' Club members are very happy about a special person and we'd like to thank her publicly. Thank you, Mrs. Gray. (A flower is presented to Mrs. Gray.)

Thank you for being such a good audience.

2. Script Used for an Assembly Program
(Betsy Bookworm, M.C.)

Hi, boys and girls. I'm Betsy Bookworm and I just love books. I'm here this morning to help Erie School celebrate Children's Book Week. I've brought a big book along with all sorts of friends inside. Shall I have them come out to see you?

(Betsy peeks in the door of the library and calls back to the audience.)

My goodness, I think I see Little Red Riding Hood and I do believe it's her Grandmother too! (Characters make an entrance.)

Chorus sings: Little Red Riding Hood, Little Red Riding Hood,
Brave little girl with a cape of red,
Brave little girl with a hood on her head.
Little Red Riding Hood, Little Red Riding Hood. .

Here's a fine looking fellow with a really great lasso. I think his name is Pecos Bill.

Chorus: (Tune of "There Was an Old Lady")
There once was a cowboy, his name Pecos Bill
The wild things he did, would give you a thrill.
He could ride broncos and lasso cyclones.
He could do even more without even a moan,
        That's Pecos Bill.

Now here's a friend for me and you. I hope he didn't bring *his* friends Thing One and Thing Two!! May I present . . . The Cat in the Hat!!

Chorus: (Tune of "Erie Canal")
I read this book about a cat, Hedodododededodedodo,
Not only that but he had a hat, Heydodododededodedodo.
He came to a house with Thing One and Thing Two.
You *just* never knew what they would do.
The name of this book I know you can guess.
The Cat in the Hat, you couldn't have missed.

(Betsy peeks in the door again.) There's something black and beautiful ready to say, "Salutations." A true friend to Wilbur . . . Can you guess who? (Pause) You're right! Let's say hello to Charlotte, a friend indeed.

Chorus: My name is Charlotte,
I live in a web.
I helped a pig named Wilbur
By thinking with my head.

Now pretend you're back in history, over a hundred years ago. Are you ready? . . . Ladies and Gentlemen, the President of the United States, Mr. Lincoln!

Chorus: (Tune of "Deep in the Heart of Texas")
When Lincoln was our President x x x x a long long time ago
He dressed so funny, it'd make you laugh hohoho - a long
   long long time ago.
His whiskers were as black as night x x x x a long long time ago.
They covered up his chin all right x x x x a long long time ago.
His coat was down around his knees x x x x a long long time ago.
His hat a stove pipe if you please x x x x a long long time ago.

Here's a happy couple coming next. I think you know them as Raggedy Ann and Andy.

Chorus: (Tune of "Twinkle Twinkle Little Star")
Two little ragdolls I once knew,
Raggedy Ann and Andy too.
They could laugh and they could run.
Believe me they had lots of fun.
(Repeated from the beginning.)

(Book jacketed student planted in audience): Boo hoo. Boo hoo. (Walks forward to stage, rubbing his eyes and sobbing.)

What's the matter little book? What's wrong? Why are you crying?

I'm a lost book. Someone checked me out from the library and didn't keep track of me. Boo hoo, boo hoo.

Oh dear, we don't want this to happen again. Here, lost book, let me help you back to storybook land so someone else can enjoy you. (Betsy assists the "book" back through the library door, peeking in again.)

Who is this beautiful lady? She looks like a princess. Why, it's Cinderella!

Chorus: Cinderella rella rella rella rella rella rella.
Shine my shoes and brush my hair then
Mop the floor and sweep the stair
Fix my nails and clean the cella
Cinderella rella rella.

Announcing the arrival of two Charlie's!

Here's Charlie Brown!

Appendixes

(Five lines from the song and musical, "You're a Good Man, Charlie Brown," were sung by the chorus.)

And here's Charlie with his Wonka's Whipple-Scrumptious Fudge-Mallow Delight!

Chorus: (Tune of "On Top of Old Smoky")
There is another Charlie you see —
Winner of a ticket, to a factory —
The group that was chosen
Were quite select
To visit the factory of chocolate.
The strange things they did
And the wonders they saw,
We just know you'll want to,
Read about it all.

Last but not least, may I present Davy Crockett. Everyone, make him feel welcome and join in his song.

(Chorus sings chorus and first verse of "Davy Crockett.")

Let's do it again! (Song is repeated.)

(All the characters now join in with the chorus to sing a farewell song.)

(Tune: "John Brown's Body")
We are, we are, we are some of your friends who live in books,
Come see, come see, come see us in the library - have a good look.
Take time, take time take time to read the pages in storybook land.
So long - we'll see you then.

(The song is repeated as the characters file back into the library.)

Goodbye boys and girls. Maybe I'll see you in a book some day.

3. Script Used for the Cat in the Hat Tryout Speech

Hi kids!! It's your old friend, Cat in the Hat, back again! Boy, do I ever love all this exposure! In fact, why don't you and I just have a little chat and we'll just forget about the rest of the celebration.

What?

You don't want to talk about ME?!!

Spoilsports!

(To students: Please plan on putting in expression and gestures that you think might be appropriate. Memorize these lines or, at least, the general ideas. Make pauses in the timing that you think are right for expression and for audience response. Good luck! And be proud of yourself for trying.)

4. Script Used for an Assembly Program (Cat in the Hat M.C.—Script A)

(Cat in the Hat comes out of the library door, cheering for himself. He taps Mr. Ethington on the shoulder.)

Mr. Ethington, I have some book friends who want to meet the students at Erie School. May I introduce them?

Boo hoo, boo hoo (from Little Bo Peep from the back of the crowd.) Boo hoo, boo hoo (Little Bo Peep cries even louder and rubs her eyes coming up front.)

Oh, what's the matter Little Bo Peep?

(Little Bo Peep, crying and talking at the same time.) I've lost my sheep! I don't know where to find them!!

(Cat in the Hat pats her on the shoulder.) There, there, Little Bo Peep. I think I saw them around the corner (pointing). Why don't you look that way?

Little Bo Peep: All right. Thank you Cat in the Hat. (Goes off looking, shading eyes with hand and peering into the distance.)

Meanwhile I'd like to introduce someone who is all ready for cold weather. (Dramatic gesture to doorway.) May I present . . . Frosty the Snowman!

(Frosty dances a little to his music.) Oh, Cat in the Hat, I have to get out of this sun! (Or, depending on the weather . . .) Oh, Cat in the Hat, I really like this cold weather . . . now I won't melt.

Frosty, you better hurry over to the shade. (Or, if the weather is cold.) I'm glad someone likes this cold weather, Frosty.

(Frosty waves goodbye and goes over to the side.)

Ooh! Who is this coming out of the book? Peter Rabbit?

No, no, Cat in the Hat, I'm the Runaway Bunny and I'm trying to run away from my mother. I have to hurry. Goodbye! (Hops to the side.)

(Cat in the Hat peeks in the book.) My goodness, I think I see a dog scatching around in there! Who are you?

Appendixes

I'm the Diggingest Dog! For a long while I couldn't dig at all but then I learned how and I dug through the gardens, I dug through the streets, and I dug through . . (The Diggingest Dog is interrupted by the Cat in the Hat.)

O.K., O.K., Diggingest Dog. Be careful and don't dig up our playground.

Now it gives me great pleasure to introduce a real buddy of mine. He was around before R2D2. Come on out . . . My Robot Buddy!

(My Robot Buddy comes out in a stiff-legged walk.) Hey, Cat in the Hat, want to climb a tree with me? I've been practicing moving my joints.

Not right now, Robot Buddy, I have more friends to introduce. Wait for me over there, O.K.?

My next friend is a wonderful beast, Aslan himself, all the way from Narnia.

(Aslan) Cat in the Hat, I came to ask the boys and girls in the fifth and sixth grades to start reading about me and my friends in *The Lion, the Witch, and the Wardrobe* and the six other chronicles of Narnia. (Aslan walks off proudly.)

Thank you for coming, Aslan . . . Ooh, I hear someone running fast. Look out, here he comes! (Runaway Ralph runs past and off the stage on the other side.) Come back and tell us who you are!

(Runaway Ralph, panting.) Don't you know, Cat in the Hat? I'm Runaway Ralph and Catso is after me! Goodbye, I really must run!!

Well, I hope the next book friend stays longer.

(Pippi taps Cat in the Hat on the back, sneaking up while he is talking.) Cat in the Hat, you're just in time to help me cut out cookies. Here, I'll roll them out right here. Hold this cookie cutter for me.

Pippi Longstocking, you can't roll out cookie dough here!

(Pippi) Why not, I always roll my cookies out on the floor and I need to get ready for Christmas.

Pippi, we haven't even had Thanksgiving yet! Your cookies can wait. (Cat in the Hat scoots Pippi off the stage.) Besides I have another friend who is just burning to meet you all. His name is . . . . . My Father's Dragon!

(My Father's Dragon) I'm on my way back to Blueland, Cat in the Hat, so I can't stay. Nice to meet everyone, though.

(Music: Mary had a little lamb)

Well, well, what do you know? Mary, it looks like you have two lambs today!

(Mary) Oh, no, Cat in the Hat. I have my own lamb and I've found Little Bo Peep's sheep, too.

(Little Bo Peep rushes up on stage and so does everyone else, with exclamations of "Oh good! Terrific! I'm so glad! Thank you, thank you, Mary!")

It's time to go back in the library. We just have time to sing our song.

>(Tune: "Twinkle, Twinkle Little Star")
>Here we are, your friends from books!
>Hope that you liked our looks.
>In the library you will find,
>Fact and fiction for your mind.
>Now we'd like for you to cheer
>For Children's Book Week now this year.

(Cat in the Hat yells.) Three cheers for books! Come on everyone!

(Leads three "hip, hip hooray" cheers.) All characters wave goodbye and enter the library.

5. Script Used for an Assembly Program (Cat in the Hat M.C. — Script B)

(Prancing music) Hi, folks! (Victory sign) Of course, you know who I am! (Pauses and cups hand behind ear to hear their response.) Louder! (Struts and acts very proud.) That's right! (Victory sign) Oh, I almost forgot . . . (tapping head) . . . Today, in honor of National Children's Book Week, I'm very pleased to present to you some old and new book characters from your library books. Our first seems to be . . . (fanfare)

a little leftover witch. Would you like to speak to these nice people, Little Leftover Witch? (Character has temper tantrum about brushing her hair.)

Oh, well. And who is this person dressed in red that I see running around in there? (Little Red Riding Hood, panting, expresses fear of the wolf.) Oh, don't you remember, Little Red Riding Hood? The woodchopper took care of him!

I think this next character must like purple. (Fanfare and Harold enters with his purple crayon and explains what he does with it.)

And we may have someone else left over from Halloween. (Georgie enters and tells everyone his name and that he is dressed like this all year long because he really *is* a ghost.)

Someone told me that a princess is coming to visit us. (Fanfare as the Princess and her Pea make an entrance.) Are you a real princess? (Character relates how she felt the pea through 20 mattresses and 20 featherbeds.)

I know the next book character is not a princess. In fact, I think she even tells lies. (Molly, from *Molly's Lies* explains her problems.)

Appendixes

Telling stories is one thing, but I remember another book character who is an intruder and enters a home when the owners aren't there.... (Fanfare and Goldilocks enters, sobbing over the broken chair she holds.)

All right, Goldilocks. Now remember, don't sit on any more small chairs. Goodbye. Oh, who are these people coming along? (Ramona appears with her mother and keeps pulling tissues from a box. They identify themselves.)

Whew! I'm glad I'm not Ramona's mother! (Pause) And now, may I present, your friend and mine.... (fanfare)... Curious George! Hi, how are you doing, George? (George, accompanied by the man with the big yellow hat, boasts about his medal prominently showing on his chest.)

Great, Curious George. Bye now. This next character is not so bold. Maybe I can talk him into coming out to see us. Come on out, Ira. We're nice people out here. (Ira and Reggie arrive clutching their Teddy bears and Ira asks the audience if he should take Tah Tah with him when he sleeps over at Reggie's house.)

Well, I hope he takes his Teddy bear. But now, I'm delighted to present... (fanfare).. Fudgie, Peter, and Alex! Can you explain these costumes? (Characters, dressed for trick or treating, do so.)

Oh, I see. Well, bye now. (Shades eyes and looks toward the back of the audience.) Now, why is that girl back there running around with boys' clothing over her arm? (Interaction with Janice Riker in which she admits stealing the clothes from Soup and Rob while they are skinny dipping.)

Well, I guess that explains why our last two book characters are dressed the way they are... (fanfare)... (Two boys appear wearing dresses and exchange insults with Janice Riker.)

(All characters crowd back and break into song.)

> (Tune: Twinkle, Twinkle Little Star)
> We are, we are your friends from books.
> Hope that you like our looks.
> When you visit the library
> Look us up, we don't cost a fee.
> Now join with us in a big hooray.
> That's how we feel about books today.

(The Cat in the Hat leads the characters and audience in three cheers.)

6. Script Used for Parade Introductions (Cat in the Hat M.C.—Script A)

(Victory sign. Prances in to Pink Panther music)

Hi, folks! (Big wave.)

Of course you know who *I* am . . .

Oh, say it louder. (Hand behind ear.)

Louder!

Wonderful! (Struts around, thumbs in armholes.)

Oh! I almost forgot. . . . I was supposed to introduce our parade today. It's National Children's Book Week and we're having a parade to celebrate it. On with the show!! (Flourish in direction of door. Fanfare from band.)

(Later in the middle of character introductions, the Cat in the Hat interrupts with . . .)

Has anyone seen Thing One and Thing Two?! I've lost them!! (Points to audience.) Let me know if you see them, O.K.?

7. Script Used for Parade Introductions (Cat in the Hat M.C.—Script B)

Ladies and gentlemen!! Welcome to a truly important celebration today in honor of National Children's Book Week. It's important because if you didn't have children's books, you wouldn't have me! Ahem. . . . How about three cheers for me. (Leads three cheers, and then struts around happily.) And now, as I was saying . . . this is a truly important . . . serious . . . solemn . . . occasion. (Is interrupted by the appearance of a truly silly character who will elicit laughter from the audience.) Oh, well, I guess we can have fun too. On with the introductions!! Here is our first grade announcer!

APPENDIX D: BOOK CELEBRATION PROGRAMS

Program A

Program for a Book Celebration with Each Class Presenting One Title

(The following was the program outline for a celebration at Erie School in which two-thirds of the classes were represented. The class presentations varied from a simple introduction of characters to short dramatizations of a single scene. Identical boaters made announcers and stage crew recognizable and official. Since we have no backstage area, short "between acts" were developed by library club members and individual teachers to maintain interest while larger groups of children were moving up to the stage area.) *A drum roll was the signal for applause for each class presentation.*

1. Fanfare

2. Cat in the Hat introduction/interaction with pedlar from Caps for Sale

3. Gingerbread Man—Mrs. Reinke's EMH Class—Sleepy pedlar falling asleep on stage

4. Very Hungry Caterpillar—Mrs. Deschenes' First Grade—Monkeys steal pedlar's caps

5. The Five Chinese Brothers—Mrs. Dugan's First Grade—Pedlar shaking finger at monkeys; monkeys shaking fingers at pedlar

6. I'm Terrific—Mrs. Rico's First Grade

7. The Enormous Egg—Mrs. Grubb's Second Grade—Pedlar stamping foot at monkeys and vice versa

8. Cloudy with a Chance of Meatballs—Mrs. Carlson's Second Grade—Pedlar throwing down his cap in disgust; monkeys duplicating his action

9. Ramona the Pest—Mrs. Williams' Second Grade—Cat in the Hat chasing Thing One and Thing Two carrying big box, the latter running through the audience and doing flips on stage. All three led the audience in a "stretch" routine.

10. Strega Nona—Mrs. Donovan's Third Grade—Bet between North Wind and Sun

11. Charlotte's Web—Mr. Slater's Third Grade—North Wind trying to blow coat off traveller

12. Harry Cat's Pet Puppy—Ms. Cantrell's Third Grade—Appearance of male sixth grade teacher dressed as Little Red Riding Hood, asking the Cat in the Hat about the Wolf and running about the stage in distress.

13. Bunnicula—Mrs. Moyers' Third Grade—Victory of Sun over North Wind (traveller takes off coat and decides to go for a swim)

14. James and the Giant Peach—Mrs. Hartman's and Mrs. Appleton's Fourth Grades—Clifford the Big Red Dog chasing The Cat in the Hat through the audience

15. Island of the Blue Dolphins—Mrs. Hardy's Fifth Grade—Same sixth grade teacher as the Wolf, looking for Little Red Riding Hood.

16. The Wish Giver—Mrs. Hodsden's Sixth Grade

17. Fanfare

18. Cheers led by The Cat in the Hat.

Program B

Program for a Book Celebration with Each Class Presenting One Title

1. Fanfare

2. Cat in the Hat introduction followed by interaction with baby bird from *Are You My Mother?* after it hatched with a flourish from a large egg on stage

3. The Little Engine that Could—Mrs. Reinke's EMH Class

4. Caps for Sale—Mrs. Betty Wilson's Kindergarten Class—Baby bird asks pedlar, "Are you my mother?"

5. Keep Your Mouth Closed, Dear—Mrs. Rico's First Grade

6. The Dragons of Blueland—Ms. Bozarth's First Grade

7. Alexander and the Terrible, Horrible, No Good, Very Bad Day—Mrs. Deschenes' First Grade Class—Baby Bird has temper tantrum about its terrible, horrible, no good, very bad day but calms down to search determinedly for its mother again

8. Ramona the Pest—Mrs. Williams' Second Grade—Cat in the Hat, Little Red Riding Hood (played by male sixth grade teacher), and baby bird interaction

9. The Karate Kid, Part II—Mrs. Donovan's Third Grade

10. Me and the Weirdos—Mr. Slater's Third Grade—Chase between the Cat in the Hat and Thing One and Thing Two, ending with their leading a stretch routine for audience participation

11. Miss Nelson Is Missing—Mrs. Nuest's Fourth Grade

12. A Wrinkle in Time—Mrs. Schaab's Fourth Grade

Appendixes

13. The Mouse and the Motorcycle—Mrs. Hardy's Fifth Grade—A cheer for R-E-A-D led by a teacher in the audience

14. The Pinballs—Mr. Bursi's Fifth Grade

15. Charlie and the Chocolate Factory—Mr. Fanucci's Fifth Grade—A cheer for B-O-O-K-S led by a second teacher in the audience

16. The Best Christmas Pageant Ever—Mrs. Hamilton's Fifth Grade

17. Snow White/Tom Sawyer—Mr. Mealka's Sixth Grade

18. The Night Walkers—Mrs. Hodsden's Sixth Grade

19. Cat in the Hat three cheers for books, followed by loud and joyful reunion of baby bird with mother bird center stage (Mother bird, complete with moustache, was played by the same sixth grade teacher as did Little Red Riding Hood.)

While classes were moving on and off stage, baby bird would sob and ask, "Are you my mother?" of a few students.

The mother bird costume was constructed by taping construction paper feathers on a white garbage bag base, as detailed in *Easy Costumes You Don't Have to Sew*. Rather than the headgear as illustrated in this title, however, a beak and a few feathers sufficed since we wanted the audience to be able to identify the teacher.

APPENDIX E: MEANDERINGS FROM MARY, THE MAD MEDIA MISTRESS

The Book Parade

Friday, November 18 - 1:00 p.m.

a. If you don't have the entry form and parade rules, please send your library rep to get same.
Deadline - Thursday, Nov 10 - Adjustment OK until Nov 14

b. Library Club members will be doing the announcing this year. If you'd like a particular script to go with your characters, please let me know. Otherwise, I'll manufacture one.

c. No ideas for costumes or floats??

—think about Mother Goose and picture story book characters, ones with easily identifiable trademarks

—ask your kids

—request a carousel of slides from previous parades from me (one day notice, please)

—request a list of characters with possible props from me (ready by Monday) or individual suggestions from me

—utilize the costume books on reserve and overnight checkout residing on my desk

—try an art period using paper bags or paper plates to make animal heads - vote on the best - use non-participants to make a large colorful title sign

d. Do remember that this is a celebration of characters from children's literature. Try to avoid characters primarily associated with TV and movies.

Parade Announcer Directions

You will be identified by your "barbershop quartet" hats. Get these from me first thing on Friday. Remove them with a flourish at the end of your part of the introductions and bow as a signal for the audience to applaud.

Gather the students from your grade level and report to the cafeteria at your scheduled time. Take attendance and line them up in order, adjusting to last minute changes. (You should have the students' names and the titles and order of your entries memorized.)

Assume the role of a teacher in terms of monitoring the behavior of your students. Times to be absolutely quiet are when you are close to the cafeteria door and while you are

Subject Index

    school to parent   125
    teacher to parent   129–130
Four-footed character   31

Glasses   31
Guessing games   86, 97–98, 100

Hats   24–26
    coolie   56
    matador   59
    Robin Hood   46
    Viking helmet   89
Headgear   18–26; *see also* Hats
    aviation   86
    boxes   22–23
    effect on audibility   97
    masks   18–20
    sacks   20–22

Illustrations; *see also* Photographs
    beak and comb (for the little red hen)   26
    beard attachment   32
    Ben Franklin bodi-puppet   30
    bodies
        bodi-puppet and arm attachment   30
        chalk   56
        Charlotte   16
        four-footed animal   31
        owl sack   20
        penguin (for Captain Cook)   27
        sandwich board (watermelon for the very hungry caterpillar)   27
        sack fitting   27
        stuffed body (by Chernoff and Hartelius)   28
    Cat in the Hat   24, 105
    caterpillar   18
    Clifford   21
    ears (rabbit)   26
    eyeholes
        Clifford   21
        ghost   22
    "feet" and shoe covers (Humbug Witch)   32
    flyer illustrations
        Humpty Dumpty   132
        Mother Goose   125
        Sam-I-Am   129
    headgear
        hats
            Cat in the Hat   24, 105
            coolie   56
            crowns   25
            duck/visor   26
            helmet (Viking)   89
            matador   59
            Robin Hood   46
            tricorn shape   25
        masks and stick puppets
            monkey   57
            mouse   18, 19
            North Wind   47
            pig, with snout   19

                    skull shape 20
                    the very hungry caterpillar 18
                nylons as base for ears and wig 23
                sacks and boxes
                    cat headgear 23
                    Clifford the big red dog 21
                    fitting of sacks and boxes 22
                    lion 20
                    owl 20
        props
            egg and feather 111
            lantern 54
            shield, Viking 89
        sign tips 33
        the very hungry caterpillar 18
        wigs 23, 31
Inanimate objects 8, 27
Introductions
        by announcer/narrators 96–98, 101, 111–121, 148–149
        by characters 96–98, 140–143
        by master of ceremonies 96–99, 136–144

Judging entries 100

Letters from students 102–104
Limitation of entries 100–101, 132–134
Lyrics 99, 137–139, 142

Make-up 31–32
        Violet Beauregarde 117
Masks 18–20
Master of Ceremonies *see* Introductions
Mini-dramatization examples 7, 69, 70, 96–97, 111–121
Mother Goose characters 38–41
Mythology characters 45, 93

Nameless characters 9
Narrated dramatizations 111–121
Newspaper reports 105–106
Non-fiction characters 93–94
Number of entries *see* Limitation of entries
Nylon stocking use 23

Pantomime 111
Parade entry forms 132–135
Parades 100–101, 148–150
Parent information forms 125, 129, 130
Photographing celebrations 2, 101, 149
Photographs
        Abraham Lincoln 87
        Arthur from *Arthur's Halloween* 17
        Berenstain bear 17
        Big Anthony 50
        Cat in the Hat 50, 106
        Charlotte 15
        Clifford 50
        Curious George 51
        Doctor De Soto 106
        dragon 49
        Frosty the Snowman 29

Subject Index

    the funny little woman 51
    Funnybones skeletons 49
    Humpty Dumpty 39
    Johnny Appleseed 87
    the knight and the dragon 49
    Library Club students 102
    Lion 84
    Little Bo Peep 39
    Little Miss Muffet 39
    Little Rabbit Who Wanted Red Wings 50
    Mary, Mary, Quite Contrary 39
    oni 51
    Owl 84
    skeletons 49
    Snow White 43
    Strega Nona 50
    the three little pigs 43
    Tigger 84
    Tin Woodman 84
    wild thing 1
    wolf 43
Picture story book characters 48–69
Poetry characters and festival 93–94
Pop-in tours 86, 98, 126
Presentations/programs *see* Book celebration programs
Props 6–14, 31–32, 35, 56; *see also* Illustrations: props

Reader practice in prop selection 7–8
Rehearsals 97, 101, 109, 110, 150
Responses to book celebrations 1, 95, 96, 97, 99, 100, 102–106, 108
Role modeling 2

Sacks 20–22
Scheduling celebrations 96, 98, 108, 126, 131, 150
School supplies 16
Script sources (commercial) 121, 124
Scripts, sample
    assembly programs 99, 117–118, 120–121, 136–143
    Cat in the Hat tryout 139–140
    individual classroom programs 96–98
    parades 143–144
    student-authored
        for *The Wish Giver* 120–121
        for *A Wrinkle in Time* 117–118
Signs 11, 12, 27, 32–33, 96, 108, 109, 149
Sources for costuming materials 15–16, 23
Stick puppets 18–20
Stocking head cover 23
Swords 32

Tails 32
Teacher information forms 106–108, 126–128
Television talk show 107
Titles for class presentations of a single title 122–124
Tryouts 101, 139–140
Tours 86, 98, 126

Wigs 23, 31
Wings 32
Women's History Week 86

AUTHOR/TITLE INDEX

Aardema, Verna 12, 62, 114
Abel's Island 69
Adams, Adrienne 12
The Adventures of Peter Rabbit 13
Aesop 45
Ahlberg, Alan 49, 67
Ahlberg, Janet 49, 67
Alexander, Lloyd 120
Alexander, Sue 55
Alexander and the Terrible, Horrible, No Good, Very Bad Day 48
Alexander Who Used to Be Rich Last Sunday 48
Alfie Gets in First 48
Alfie's Feet 52
Alice's Adventures in Wonderland 13, 70
Aliki 56, 87
Allard, Harry 12, 64, 112
Alvin, Beth 94
Amelia Bedelia 52
Anatole 52
And My Mean Old Mother Will Be Sorry, Blackboard Bear 55
An Anteater Named Arthur 53
Are You My Mother? 146
Arthur's Halloween 17 (photo), 52
Arthur's Halloween Costume 52
Arthur's Valentine 52
Asch, Frank 53, 66
Ask Mr. Bear 111
Atwater, Richard 78

"Baa, Baa, Black Sheep" 38
Bags Are Big! A Paper Bag Craft Book 21, 31
Bailey, Carolyn 12
Balian, Lorna 11
Banks, Lynne Reid 79
A Bargain for Frances 57
Barrett, Judi 65
Barry, Robert 65
Bate, Lucy 7, 13
Bauer, Caroline Feller 121
Baum, L. Frank 73
Bea and Mr. Jones 53
The Bears' Christmas 17 (photo), 54
Bears in the Night 54
The Bears' Vacation 54
The Bed Just So 67
Bedford, Annie 60
Beezus and Ramona 71
Benji in Business 71
Berenstain, Jan 17, 54

Berenstain, Stan 17, 54
Best Friends for Frances 59
Big Bear Goes Fishing 55
Big Bear to the Rescue 55
The Bionic Bunny Show 13
Bishop, Claire Huchet 56
The Black Cauldron 120
Blackboard Bear 55
Blubber 72
The Blue-Nosed Witch 12
Blume, Judy 9, 69, 70, 72, 75
Bonne, Rose 66
Bonsall, Crosby 68
The Boy Who Turned into a TV Set 79
Bread and Jam for Frances 59
"The Bremen Town Musicians" 42
Bridwell, Norman 37, 50
Bright, Robert 7, 9
Bringing the Rain to Kapiti Plain 62
Brittain, Bill 120
Brown, Laurene Krasny 13
Brown, Marc 13, 18, 48, 52
Brown, Margaret Wise 13
Bunnicula 72
Burningham, John 65
Byars, Betsy 73

Caps for Sale 20, 25, 66
Carle, Eric 61, 68, 93
Carlson, Carol 18 (illus)
Carroll, Lewis 12, 70
The Case of the Hungry Stranger 68
The Cat Ate My Gymsuit 77
The Cat in the Hat 50 (photo), 55, 106 (photo)
The Cat in the Hat Comes Back 55
The Chalk Box Story 48, 56
The Champion of Merrimack County 79
Champlin, Connie 30, 35, 85, 121
"Characterization in Literature: Realistic and Historical Fiction" 107
Charlie and the Chocolate Factory 73, 114, 116, 124
Charlotte's Web 2 (photo), 16, 74, 114, 115
Chernoff, Goldie 4, 21, 28, 29, 35, 36, 59
Children's Literature in the Reading Program 107
"Cinderella" 42, 113
Claude the Dog, a Christmas Story 57
Cleary, Beverly 7, 8, 11, 69, 71, 74, 77, 80, 81
Clifford the Big Red Dog 57
Clifford's Family 50 (photo)
Clifford's Halloween 57
Cloudy with a Chance of Meatballs 8, 65

Author/Title Index

Coerr, Eleanor 86
Cole, William 94
Coombs, Patricia 11
Corduroy 57
Costumes for Plays and Playing 37
"The Country Mouse and the City Mouse" 44
Cox, Marcia 36
Creature Costumes 36
The Cricket in Times Square 73
Crictor 64
Cullinan, Bernice (ed.) 107
Curious George 57
Curious George Gets a Medal 57
Curious George Goes to the Hospital 51 (photo), 58
Curious George Rides a Bike 57
Curious George Takes a Job 57
The Cut-Ups 58
The Cybil War 73

Dahl, Roald 10, 73, 75
"Dainty Dottie Dee" 93
Danny and the Dinosaur 58, 97
Danziger, Paula 8, 72, 77
Days with Frog and Toad 59
"Deaf Donald" 93
Dear Mr. Henshaw 77
DeClements, Barthe 74
De Paola, Tomie 49, 50, 55, 63
Devlin, Wende 11
The Diggingest Dog 58
Disney, Walt 46, 86, 113
Doctor De Soto 58, 106 (photo)
Dr. Seuss' ABC 68
Dorrie and the Blue Witch 11
Dorrie and the Witch's Imp 11
The Dragon Halloween Party 37
Drury, Roger 79
DuBois, William Pené 48, 63

The Easter Egg Artists 12
Easy Costumes You Don't Have to Sew 4, 21, 36, 147
Easy to Make Costumes 22, 36
Easy to Make Monster Masks and Disguises 36
Eisner, Vivienne 32, 36
Ellen Tebbits 74
Embry, Margaret 12
The Enormous Egg 31
Ets, Marie Hall 38

Fatio, Louise 61
Feller, Marsha 18
Feller, Ron 18
Fisk, Nicholas 75
Fitzgerald, John 82
The Five Chinese Brothers 56
Flack, Marjorie 111
Fourth Grade Celebrity 72
Freckle Juice 70
Freeman, Don 56, 57
Frog and Toad are Friends 60

Frog and Toad Together 60
Frosty the Snowman 29 (photo), 60
The Funny Little Woman 51 (photo), 60
Funnybones 20 (illus), 49 (photos), 67

Gackenbach, Dick 48, 57, 62
Gag, Wanda 113
Galdone, Paul 43, 45
Gannett, Ruth Stiles 74
Gates, Frieda 22, 36
George, Jean 76, 82
George and Martha 2, 48, 60, 96–97
George and Martha Encore 60
George and Martha Rise and Shine 60
Georgie and the Noisy Ghost 9
Georgie and the Robbers 9
Georgie Goes West 9
Georgie's Halloween 9
The Ghost with the Halloween Hiccups 10
Giff, Patricia Reilly 72
Gilbreath, Alice 36
"The Gingerbread Man" 44
Glovach, Linda 37
"Goldilocks" 44
The Great Brain Reforms 82
Green Eggs and Ham 129
Grinny 75
The Grouchy Ladybug 61
Grubb, Nancy 21 (illus)
The Guinness Book of World Records 136
The Gunniwolf 8, 63
Gus was a Friendly Ghost 10
Gus was a Gorgeous Ghost 7, 10

Haley, Gail 35, 37
Halloween with Morris and Boris 10, 55
"Hansel and Gretel" 44
The Happy Lion 61
Hardendorff, Jeanne 67
"The Hare and the Tortoise" 13, 44
Harold and the Purple Crayon 8, 61, 85, 96
Harold's Trip to the Sky 61
Harper, Wilhemina 8, 63
Harry and the Lady Next Door 61
Harry the Dirty Dog 61
Hartelius, Margaret 4, 21, 28, 29, 36
"Hey, Diddle, Diddle" 38
"Hickory, Dickory, Dock" 40
Hinton, S. E. 81
Hoban, Lillian 52
Hoban, Russell 6, 8, 59
Hoff, Syd 58
Hogrogian, Nonny 59
Homer the Hunter 9
Horton Hatches an Egg 61
Horton Hears a Who 62
Hound and Bear 48, 62
The House at Pooh Corner 84 (photo)
The How and Why Wonder Book of Butterflies and Moths 93

How to Eat Fried Worms 71, 119
How to Eat Fried Worms: and Other Plays 119
Howe, James 72
Hughes, Shirley 52
Humbug Witch 11
"Humpty Dumpty" 39 (photo), 40
Hurd, Edith Thacher 62
Hutchins, Pat 6

I Know an Old Lady Who Swallowed a Fly 66
I Sure am Glad to See You, Blackboard Bear 55
The Indian in the Cupboard 79
Ira Sleeps Over 62

"Jack and Jill" 40
"Jack and the Beanstalk" 44, 45
"Jack Be Nimble" 40
James and the Giant Peach 10, 16, 75, 124
Janice 63
Jelly Belly 76, 85
"Jimmy Jet and his TV Set" 93
Johnny Appleseed, The Story of 87 (photo)
Johnny Lion's Bad Day 62
Johnny Lion's Boots 62
Johnson, Crockett 61
Julie of the Wolves 76
Jumanji 80
Jump, Frog, Jump 59
Just Like Daddy 53

Kalan, Robert 59
Katy No-Pocket 62
Keats, Ezra Jack 66
Keep Your Mouth Closed, Dear 56, 128
Keller, Helen 90
"King Midas and the Golden Touch" 45
A Kiss for Little Bear 63
The Knight and the Dragon 49 (photos), 63

Laughlin, Florence 12
"Lazy Jane" 93
Lazy Tommy Pumpkinhead 48, 63
Leaf, Munro 58
Lear, Edward 94
Learning Magazine 86
Leedy, Loreen 37
Left-Handed Shortstop 72
L'Engle, Madeleine 117
Lentil 8, 63
Lewis, C. S. 2, 70
Lindgren, Astrid 80
Lindgren, Barbro 68
"The Lion and the Mouse" 45
The Lion, the Witch, and the Wardrobe 70, 141
Little Bear Marches in the St. Patrick's Day Parade 35, 63
Little Bear's Thanksgiving 63
"Little Bo Peep" 39 (photo), 40
"Little Boy Blue" 40
Little House in the Big Woods 77

The Little Leftover Witch 12
"Little Miss Muffet" 39 (photo), 40
The Little Old Lady Who Was Not Afraid of Anything 64
The Little Rabbit Who Wanted Red Wings 12, 50 (photo)
Little Rabbit's Loose Tooth 7, 13, 127, 130
"The Little Red Hen" 45
"Little Red Riding Hood" 45
The Little Witch's Black Magic Book of Disguises 37
Lobel, Arnold 60
Lord, John 8
"The Loser" 93

MacDonald, Betty 78
Making Costumes for Parties, Plays, and Holidays 36
Making Paper Costumes 36
Manes, Stephen 79
Margolis, Richard 10, 55
Marshall, James 48, 58, 60
"Mary Had a Little Lamb" 40
"Mary, Mary Quite Contrary" 39 (photo), 40
Mary Poppins 78
McCall's 35
McCloskey, Robert 8, 63
McEwan, Elaine K. 86
Merrill, Jean 74
Mexico from A to Z 94
Miles, Betty 77
Millions of Cats 113
Milne, A. A. 73, 83
Minarik, Else 63
Miss Nelson is Missing 64
Mr. Gumpy's Outing 65
Mr. Popper's Penguins 78
Mr. Rabbit and the Lovely Present 13
"Mr. Smeds and Mr. Spats" 94
Mr. Willowby's Christmas Tree 65
Mrs. Piggle-Wiggle 78
The Mitten 8, 61
Mitzi and the Elephants 78
Molly's Lies 142
Monson, Diane 107
Mooser, Stephen 9
More from Hound and Bear 62
Morris and Boris 55
Morris Has a Cold 55
Morris Tells Boris Mother Moose Stories and Rhymes 55
Mosel, Arlene 8, 51, 60
Mother Goose 39
Mother Holly 45
Mother, Mother, I Want Another 48, 53, 113
The Mouse and the Motorcycle 81, 95
Murphy, Jim 94
My Father's Dragon 74
My Side of the Mountain 82

Nate the Great 65
No Roses for Harry 61
Nobody Knows I Have Delicate Toes 54

Author/Title Index

"The North Wind and the Sun" 47, 145–146
Nothing's Fair in Fifth Grade 74

Old Black Witch 4, 11
Old Black Witch Rescues Halloween 11
"Old King Cole" 41
"The Old Woman and Her Pig" 45
One Fine Day 59
Operation: Dump the Chump 80
Organization for Equal Education of the Sexes, Inc. 86
Otis Spofford 80
The Outsiders 81
"The Owl and the Pussy Cat" 94

Paper Masks and Puppets for Stories, Songs, and Plays 18
Parish, Peggy 52
Park, Barbara 80
Patz, Nancy 54
"Paul Bunyan" 45
Payne, Emma 62
Peck, Robert Newton 10, 15, 82
Perkins, Al 58
"Peter, Peter, Pumpkin Eater" 41
Peter's Chair 66
The Piggy in the Puddle 66
Pippi Longstocking 80
The Pistachio Prescription 8, 72
Play Ball, Amelia Bedelia 52
Play with Me 38
A Pocket for Corduroy 57
Poem Stew 94
Polushkin, Maria 53, 113
Pomerantz, Charlotte 66
Popcorn 66
Potter, Beatrix 13
"Practically Speaking" 86, 94
Prelutsky, Jack 93
Presenting Reader's Theater: Plays and Poems to Read Aloud 121
The Princess and Froggie 60
"The Princess and the Pea" 46
Pumpernickle Tickle and Mean Green Cheese 23, 54
The Pumpkin Giant 81
The Pushcart War 74
"Puss in Boots" 46

"The Queen of Eene" 93
"The Queen of Hearts" 41
Quick and Easy Holiday Costumes 36

Ramona Quimby, Age 8 82
Ramona the Pest 11, 81
Rawls, Wilson 76
Renfro, Nancy 21, 30, 31, 35, 37, 85, 121
Rey, H. A. 51, 57
Robertson, Jane 94
"Robin Hood, [Some Merry Adventures of]" 46
"Rock-a-Bye Baby" 38

Rockwell, Thomas 71, 119
Rodgers, Mary 70
Runaway Bunny 13

Sachar, Louis 78
Sadako and the Thousand Paper Cranes 86
Sam 67
Sand Cake 53
"Sarah Cynthia Sylvia Stout Would Not Take the Garbage Out" 94
School Library Journal 86, 94
Schwartz, Amy 53
Scott, Ann Herbert 67
The Secret Life of the Underwear Champ 77
Selden, George 73
Sendak, Maurice 1, 64
Seuss, Dr. 25, 55, 62, 67, 68, 129
"The Seven Sneezes of Cecil Snedde" 93
Sharmat, Marjorie Weinman 65
Sherick, Janice 100
"Sick" 94
Sideways Stories from Wayside School 78
Silverstein, Shel 93
Simplicity 35
"Sitter" 94
Slobodkina, Esphyr 66
Smith, Renee vii
Smith, Robert 76
"Sneaky Pete" 94
The Sneetches and Other Stories 67
"Snow White" 43 (photo), 46, 113
A Snowy Day 66
The Soccer Book 93
Soup and Me 10, 15, 82, 119
Star Wars 86
Steig, William 58, 69
Stevenson, Robert Louis 94
The Story of Ferdinand 58
The Story of Johnny Appleseed 87 (photo)
The Story of My Life 90
Storytelling with Puppets 30, 35, 85, 121
Strega Nona 50 (photo), 54, 98
The Stupids Have a Ball 12
Summer of the Monkeys 76
Summer Switch 70
Superfudge 9
A Sweetheart for Valentine 8

Tabs 86
The Tale of Thomas Meade 6
Tales of a Fourth Grade Nothing 8, 75, 115
Thayer, Jane 7, 10
"There Was a Crooked Man" 38
"There Was an Old Woman Who Lived in a Shoe" 41
"The Three Bears" 44
"The Three Billy Goats Gruff" 46
"The Three Little Kittens" 41
The Three Little Pigs 43 (photo), 46
"The Three Wishes" 47

Travers, Pamela L. 78
Tresselt, Alvin 8, 61
Tudor, Tasha 39

Ungerer, Tomi 64

Van Allsburg, Chris 80
Van Leeuwen, Jean 71
The Very Hungry Caterpillar 27, 68, 112
Viorst, Judith 48

Waber, Bernard 53, 62
Wacky Wednesday 112
Weird and Wacky Inventions 94
We're in Big Trouble, Blackboard Bear 55
Where the Wild Things Are 1 (photo), 2, 64
Whistle for Willie 66
White, E. B. 74, 115
Who's in Rabbit's House? 12

Why Mosquitoes Buzz in People's Ears 114
Wild Animals 2
The Wild Baby 68
Wilder, Laura Ingalls 77
Wilkin, Mary E. 81
Williams, Barbara 78
Williams, Linda 64
Wilson, Betty 20, 25, 57 (illus)
"The Wind and the Sun" 47, 145–146
Winnie-the-Pooh 73, 83
Wiseman, Bernard 10, 55
The Wish Giver 120
The Witches 75, 110
The Wizard of Oz 73, 84 (photo)
A Wrinkle in Time 117

Zion, Gene 61
Zemach, Harve 60
Zolotow, Charlotte 13

Character Name/Character Type Index

    Mama Bear in *The Bears' Vacation* 54
    Mr. Bear in *Ask Mr. Bear* 111
    Papa Bear in *The Bears' Christmas* 54
    the three bears 44
    Winnie-the-Pooh 83
the beautiful butterfly in *The Very Hungry Caterpillar* 68
bee in *The Story of Ferdinand* 58–59
Beezus 71
Ben/Ape Face 70
Ben/the wild baby 68
Benjamin 54
Benjy 54
the Berenstain Bears 17 (photo), 54
Big Anthony 50 (photo), 54
Big Bear 55
the biggest bear 35
Bill Andrews (in Ape Face's body) 70
Billy 71
the Billy Goats Gruff 46
biographical characters 85–92
the Bionic Bunny 13
bird 147; *see also* baby bird; chickens; crow; duck; eagle; goose; hen; Maizie-bird; owl; penguin; redbird; rooster; sparrow
the black sheep 38
Blackboard Bear 55
Blubber 72
the Blue-Nosed Witch 12
boa constrictor (Crictor) 64
Boris 55
the Bremen Town musicians 42
brick house 46
bull (Ferdinand) 58–59
Bunnicula 72
butterfly, beautiful 68

calf in *Mr. Gumpy's Outing* 65
Captain Cook in *Mr. Popper's Penguins* 27 (illus), 78
Captain Hooper in *Georgie and the Noisy Ghost* 9–10
Casey Valentine 72
Cassie Stephens 72
cat
    bibliography 34
    Cat in *Mr. Gumpy's Outing* 65
    the Cat in the Hat 24 (hat illus), 50 (photo), 55, 105 (drawing), 106 (photo)
    Catso in *Runaway Ralph* 81
    Chester in *Bunnicula* 72
    Fred in *Humbug Witch* 11
    Gink in the Dorrie books 11
    Harry Cat in *The Cricket in Times Square* series 73
    headgear 23 (illus)
    Herman in the Georgie books 9
    in "The Bremen Town Musicians" 42
    in "Hey, Diddle, Diddle" 38
    in "I Know an Old Lady" 66
    in "The Little Red Hen" 45
    in "The Owl and the Pussy-Cat" 94
    Paw Paw in *The Cybil War* 73
    Puss in Boots 46
    the Three Little Kittens and their mother 41
Cat in the Hat 24 (hat illus), 50 (photo), 55, 105 (drawing), 106 (photo)

caterpillar
   in *The Very Hungry Caterpillar* 18 (illus), 68
   in *Who's in Rabbit's House?* 12
Centipede in *James and the Giant Peach* 75–76
chalks 56 (illus)
Charles 56, 128
Charlie 73, 116
Charlotte 15 (photo), 16 (illus), 115
Chester 73
chickens in *Mr. Gumpy's Outing* 65
chimpanzee
   Arthur 52–53
   Jimbo in *Summer of the Monkeys* 76
Chinese Brothers 56 (illus)
Christopher Robin 73, 83
Cinderella 42
City Mouse 44
Claude (the dog) 57
Clifford 21 (illus), 50 (photo), 57
clock, *see* grandfather clock
clothing items (shoes, pants, shirt, gloves, top hat) in *The Little Old Lady Who Was Not Afraid of Anything* 64
cloud in *Bringing the Rain to Kapiti Plain* 62
Cloud Men 10
clown (father in *Popcorn*) 66–67
Corduroy 57
Country Mouse 44
cow
   in *Bringing the Rain to Kapiti Plain* 62
   in "The Gingerbread Man" 44
   in "Hey, Diddle, Diddle" 38
   in *One Fine Day* 59
   see also bull; calf; ox
crayon in *Harold and the Purple Crayon* 61
cricket (Chester) 73
Crictor 64
crocodile (Charles) 56, 128
Crocodile in *My Father's Dragon* 74
crooked man 38
crow in *Why Mosquitoes Buzz in People's Ears* 114
cupcake in *The Very Hungry Caterpillar* 68, 112
Curious George 23 (cap illus), 51 (photo), 57 (mask illus)
Cut-Ups 58
Cybil Ackerman 73

Daisy in *Summer of the Monkeys* 76
Danny
   in *Ask Mr. Bear* 111
   in *Danny and the Dinosaur* 58
Darwin in the Mitzi series 78
devil
   in *Clifford's Halloween* 57
   in *Popcorn* 66–67
the diggingest dog 58
dinosaur in *Danny and the Dinosaur* 58
Doctor De Soto 58, 106 (photo)
doctor
   Dr. Skinny in *Jelly Belly* 76
   hospital personnel in *Curious George Goes to the Hospital* 58
dog
   bibliography 34
   Claude and Bummer 57

Character Name/Character Type Index

    Clifford   21 (illus), 50 (photo), 57
    the diggingest dog (Duke)   58
    Dog in *Mr. Gumpy's Outing*   65
    Fang in *Nate the Great*   65
    Harold in *Bunnicula*   72
    Harry the dirty dog   61
    Hound in *Hound and Bear*   62
    in "The Bremen Town Musicians"   42
    in "The Country Mouse and the City Mouse"   44
    in "I Know an Old Lady"   66
    in "The Little Red Hen"   45
    Kitty in the Stupids series   112
    Miss Vicki in *The Cybil War*   73
    Mop in *The Case of the Hungry Stranger*   68
    Old Rowdy in *Summer of the Monkeys*   76
    Ribsy in *Henry Huggins*   7, 69
    skeleton in *Funnybones*   67
    T-Bone in *The Cybil War*   73
    Toto in *The Wizard of Oz*   73
    Turtle in *Tales of a Fourth Grade Nothing*   115
    Willie in *Whistle for Willie*   66
donkey (Eeyore)   73
Donkey in *The Bremen Town Musicians*   42
Donkey, Mrs., in *Mother, Mother, I Want Another*   53
Dorothy   73
Dorrie   11
dragon
    in *The Ghost with the Halloween Hiccups*   10
    in *The Knight and the Dragon*   49 (photo), 63
duck (Miss Puddle Duck in *The Little Rabbit Who Wanted Red Wings*)   12–13, 26
Duck, Mrs., in *Mother, Mother I Want Another*   53
dwarves, the seven   46

eagle in *Bringing the Rain to Kapiti Plain*   62
Earthworm in *James and the Giant Peach*   75–76
Eeyore   73
egg (Humpty Dumpty)   39 (photo), 40, 132 (illus)
El in *Pumpernickle Tickle and Mean Green Cheese*   54
elephant
    El   54
    Horton   61
    in *Mitzi and the Elephants*   78–79
Ellen Tebbits   74
Elmer   74
Elsie Edwards   74

falcon (Frightful)   82
farmer, *see* under adult characters: *Charlotte's Web*, "The Gingerbread Man," *Little House in the Big Woods*, *Soup and Me*, *The Wish Giver*
feather
    in *Ask Mr. Bear*   111
    in *Bringing the Rain to Kapiti Plain*   62
Felina   12
Ferdinand   58–59
Fern   74
fiddle in "Hey, Diddle, Diddle"   38
field in *One Fine Day*   59
firefly (Glow-worm in *James and the Giant Peach*)   75–76
Fish in *Big Bear Goes Fishing*   55
fish in *Jump, Frog, Jump*   59
The Five Chinese Brothers   56

fly
  in *I Know an Old Lady* 66
  in *Jump, Frog, Jump* 59
fox
  in *Doctor De Soto* 58
  in *One Fine Day* 59
Frances 59
Frank the Flower 74–75
frog
  Frog in Frog and Toad stories 59–60
  Froggie in *The Princess and Froggie* 60
  Gower Glackens in *Abel's Island* 69–70
  in *Jump, Frog, Jump* 59
  Mrs. Frog in *Mother, Mother, I Want Another* 53
Froggie 60
Frosty the Snowman 29 (photo), 60
Fudge 9, 75, 115
the funny little woman 51 (photo), 60
"Funnybones" 20 (illus), 49 (photos), 67

George and Martha 60, 96
Georgie 9–10
ghost
  Boris 10
  Cloud Men 10
  costume 22 (illus)
  Fudge 9
  Georgie 9
  Gus 10
  Mr. Penny 10
  Rabbit 10
  Rob 10
Giant (The Pumpkin Giant) 81
giant in *Jack and the Beanstalk* 44–45
the giant jam sandwich 8
the Gingerbread Man 44
Glow-worm in *James and the Giant Peach* 75–76
goat
  Goat in *Mr. Gumpy's Outing* 65
  in *Ask Mr. Bear* 111
  in "I Know an Old Lady" 66
Goats in "The Three Billy Goats Gruff" 46, 112–113
Goldilocks 44
goose in *Ask Mr. Bear* 111
Gorilla in *My Father's Dragon* 74
grandfather clock
  in "Cinderella" 42, 113
  in "Hickory, Dickory, Dock" 40
Grandfather Stupid 12, 112
Grandmamma 75
grandparents, *see* adult characters: *Charlie and the Chocolate Factory, Jelly Belly,* "Little Red Riding Hood," *Strega Nona*
grass in *Bringing the Rain to Kapiti Plain* 62
grasshopper (Old Green Grasshopper in *James and the Giant Peach*) 75–76
Great Aunt Emma 75
the Great Brain 82
Gretel 44
the grouchy ladybug 61
groundhog (Mr. Groundhog in *The Little Rabbit Who Wanted Red Wings*) 12–13
the Gunniwolf 63–64
Gus 10

Character Name/Character Type Index

Hansel and Gretel 44
the Happy Lion 61
Hare 44
Harold 61, 72
Harry the Dirty Dog 61
hen
    in *Ask Mr. Bear* 59
    in "The Little Red Hen" 45
Henry Huggins 7, 69
hippopotamus (George and Martha) 60, 96
horse
    in "I Know an Old Lady" 66
    Little Lightning in *Georgie Goes West* 9
    Spotted Pony in *Big Bear to the Rescue* 55
Horton 61–62
Hound 62
Humbug Witch 11, 32 (illus)
Humpty Dumpty 39 (photo), 40, 132 (illus)

ice cream cone 112
iguana in *Why Mosquitoes Buzz in People's Ears* 114
inanimate object/natural phenomenon, *see* apple; beanpole; brick house; chalks; clothing items (shoes, pants, shirt, gloves, top hat); cloud; crayon; cupcake; feather; fiddle; field; giant jam sandwich; gingerbread house; grandfather clock; grass; ice cream cone; moon; pea; peach; pickle; pumpkin; rain; spoon; stream; sun; watermelon slice; and wind
Indian *see* Native American
insect *see* bee; butterfly; caterpillar; cricket; firefly; fly; grasshopper; ladybug; mosquito; spider; and wasp
Ira 62

Jack and Jill 40
Jack ("Jack and the Beanstalk") 44–45
Jack ("Jack Be Nimble") 40
jack o'lantern, *see* pumpkin
James 75
Janet in *The Champion of Merrimack County* 79
Janice Riker in the *Soup* series 15, 82, 119
Jay Berry 76
Jelly Belly 76
Jizo Sama in *The Funny Little Woman* 60
Johnny Appleseed 86, 87 (photo), 88
Johnny Lion 62
Judy in *Jumanji* 80
Julie 76

Kangaroo (Katy) 62
Kapit 62
Kapu 76
Katy No-Pocket 62
king
    Billy in *Popcorn* 66–67
    crown (illus) 25
    in *The Princess and Froggie* 60
    in *The Pumpkin Giant* 81
    King Cole 41
    King Midas 45
the Knave of Hearts 41
the knight 49 (photo), 63

Ladybug in *James and the Giant Peach* 75–76
ladybug, the grouchy 61
Larry Pryor 77

Laura Ingalls Wilder 77
Lazy Tommy Pumpkinhead 63
Leigh Botts 77
Lentil 63
lion
    Aslan 70–71
    bibliography 34–35
    Happy Lion and Lionness 61
    in *Jumanji* 80
    in *The Wizard of Oz* 73, 84 (photo)
    Johnny Lion, Father and Mother 62
    King Lion in *Why Mosquitoes Buzz in People's Ears* 114
    Lion in Aesop's "The Lion and the Mouse" 45
    sack headgear 20 (illus)
Lisa in *Corduroy* 57
Little Bear
    in titles by Janice 35, 63
    in *A Kiss for Little Bear* 63
Little Bo Peep 39 (photo), 40
Little Boy Blue 40
little bunny in *The Runaway Bunny* 13
Little Girl in *The Gunniwolf* 63–64
the little leftover witch 12
Little Miss Muffet 39 (photo), 40
the little old lady who was not afraid of anything 64
Little Rabbit
    in *The Little Rabbit Who Wanted Red Wings* 12–13, 50 (photo)
    in *Little Rabbit's Loose Tooth* 13
the little red hen 26 (illus), 45
Little Red Riding Hood 45

Madame Bodot 64
maiden in *One Fine Day* 59
Maizie-bird in *Horton Hatches an Egg* 61
Mama Bear
    in *Just Like Daddy* 53
    in "The Three Bears" 44
mammal, *see* aardvark; anteater; bat; bear; bull; calf; cat; chimpanzee; cow; dog; donkey; elephant; fox; groundhog; hare; kangaroo; goat; gorilla; hippopotamus; horse; lion; monkey; moose; mouse; ox; pig; poodle; porcupine; rabbit; rat; rhinoceros; sheep; skunks; squirrel; wolf; and zebra
the man in the big yellow hat 51 (photo), 58
Marcy Lewis 77–78
Martha and George 60, 96
Mary in "Mary Had a Little Lamb" 40
Mary in "Mary, Mary, Quite Contrary" 39 (photo), 40
Mary Ingalls 77
Mary Poppins 78
matador in *The Story of Ferdinand* 58–59 (illus)
Max 64
Maxie Hammerman in *The Pushcart War* 74–75
McBean in *The Sneetches* 67
Midas, King 45
miller in *One Fine Day* 59
Miss Muffet 40
Miss Nelson 64
Miss Puddle Duck in *The Little Rabbit Who Wanted Red Wings* 12–13
Miss Viola Swamp 64
Mr. Bear in *Ask Mr. Bear* 111
Mr. Bushy Tail in *The Little Rabbit Who Wanted Red Wings* 12–13
Mr. Groundhog 12–13

Character Name/Character Type Index

Mr. Gumpy 65
Mr. Jones 53–54
Mr. Nilsson in *Pippi Longstocking* 80–81
Mr. Penny 10
Mr. Popper 78
Mr. Rabbit in *Mr. Rabbit and the Lovely Present* 13
Mr. Willowby 65
Mr. Wonka 116
Mrs. Donkey in *Mother, Mother, I Want Another* 53, 113
Mrs. Duck 53, 113
Mrs. Frog 53, 113
Mrs. Gorf 78
Mrs. Pig in *Mother, Mother, I Want Another* 53, 113
Mrs. Piggle-Wiggle 78
Mrs. Porcupine in *The Little Rabbit Who Wanted Red Wings* 12–13
Mitzi 78
Miyax 76
monsters
    crones Ooddu, Orwen, and Orgoch in *The Black Cauldron* 12–13
    ghouls, hags, and ogres in *The Lion, the Witch, and the Wardrobe* 70–71
    the wicked *oni* in *The Funny Little Woman* 60
    the wild things in *Where the Wild Things Are* 64
monkey
    Curious George 23 (illus), 51 (photo), 57 (illus)
    in *Why Mosquitoes Buzz in People's Ears* 114
    mask 57 (illus)
    Mr. Nilsson in *Pippi Longstocking* 80
monkeys in *Caps for Sale* 20, 25, 66, 145
moon in "Hey, Diddle, Diddle" 38
Morris 10, 55
mosquito in *Why Mosquitoes Buzz in People's Ears* 114
Mother Holly 45
Mother Owl in *Why Mosquitoes Buzz in People's Ears* 114
mother, *see* many characters listed under adult characters
moose (Morris) 10, 55
mouse
    Abel 69
    Anatole 52
    baby mouse and mother 53, 113
    bibliography 35
    Country Mouse and City Mouse 44
    Doctor De Soto and wife 58
    in "Hickory, Dickory, Dock" 40
    in *The Little Red Hen* (Galdone version) 45
    mouse boy in *The Witches* 75
    Mouse in *Gus Was a Friendly Ghost* 10
    O Crispin 79
    Ralph 81
    Squeaky from Little Bear titles 63
    stick puppet 18 (illus), 19 (illus)
    Tucker in *The Cricket in Times Square* series 73
my grandfather in *The Mitten* 61

Nate the Great 65
Native American
    in *The Indian in the Cupboard* 79
    Kio in *Georgie Goes West* 9
non-fiction characters 93; *see also* biographical characters; poetry characters

O Crispin 79
Ogden Pettibone 79

Old Black Witch   11
Old Green Grasshopper in *James and the Giant Peach*   75–76
Old King Cole   41
Old Sneep in *Lentil*   63
old woman
    in "The Gingerbread Man"   44
    in "The Old Woman and Her Pig"   45
    in *One Fine Day*   59
    in "There Was an Old Woman Who Lived in a Shoe"   41
Omri   79–80
oni in *The Funny Little Woman*   51 (photo), 60
Oompa-Loompas   117
Orson Abbott   12
Oscar Winkle   80
Otis Spofford   80
the Outsiders   81
owl
    in *Bears in the Night*   54
    in *Johnny Lion's Bad Day*   62
    Miss Oliver in the Georgie series   9
    Mother Owl in *Why Mosquitoes Buzz in People's Ears*   114
    Owl in *Little Bear's Thanksgiving*   63
    sack headgear   20 (illus)
ox (Babe from Paul Bunyan)   45

Papa Bear
    in *Just Like Daddy*   53
    in "The Three Bears"   44
parent, *see* adult characters
Patroclus in *The Pumpkin Giant*   81
Patsy in *Mrs. Piggle-Wiggle*   78
Paul Bunyan   45
pea in "The Princess and the Pea"   28 (illus), 46
peach in *James and the Giant Peach*   75–76
pedlar
    in *Caps for Sale*   25, 66, 145
    in *One Fine Day*   59
penguin in *Mr. Popper's Penguins*   27 (illus), 68
Peter
    in *Jumanji*   80
    in "Peter, Peter, Pumpkin Eater"   41
    in *Peter's Chair* and *Whistle for Willie*   66
    in *Tales of a Fourth Grade Nothing* and *Superfudge*   9, 75, 115
Peter Rabbit   13
pickle in *The Very Hungry Caterpillar*   27, 68
pig
    in "The Gingerbread Man"   44
    in "The Old Woman and Her Pig"   45
    in "The Three Little Pigs"   43 (photo), 46
    Pig in *Mr. Gumpy's Outing*   65
    piggy in *The Piggy in the Puddle*   66
    Piglet in *Winnie-the-Pooh*   73–74
    stick puppet with snout   19
piggy   66
Piglet   73–74
Pippi Longstocking   80–81
poetry characters   93–94
Polly Kemp in *The Wish Giver*   120–121
Pony Boy   81
poodle (Miss Vicki in *The Cybil War*)   73

Character Name/Character Type Index

porcupine (Mrs. Porcupine in *The Little Rabbit Who Wanted Red Wings*) 12–13
preschool characters (human)
    Alfie books (Alfie and Mary Rose) 48
    Beezus and Ramona (children at Ramona's birthday party) 71
    The Case of the Hungry Stranger (Snitch) 68
    Mitzi books (Darwin) 141
    Peter's Chair/Whistle for Willie (Peter) 66
    Sam (Sam) 67
    Tales of a Fourth Grade Nothing (Ralph, Jennie, and Sam at Fudge's birthday party) 115
    The Wild Baby (the wild baby) 68
    see also Anthony in Blackboard Bear titles 55; Benjamin in *Pumpernickle Tickle and Mean Green Cheese* 54
the princess and the pea 46
the Pumpkin Giant 81
pumpkin
    in *The Little Old Lady Who Was Not Afraid of Anything* 64
    in "Peter, Peter, Pumpkin Eater" 41
the purple crayon, 61, 85
Puss in Boots 46
python in *Why Mosquitoes Buzz in People's Ears* 114

the Queen of Hearts 41

rabbit
    Bunnicula 72
    ears 26 (illus)
    Grandfather Stupid 12, 112
    Hare 44
    little bunny in *The Runaway Bunny* 13
    Little Rabbit who wanted red wings and mother 12
    Little Rabbit with the loose tooth, her parents, and tooth fairy 13
    Mr. Rabbit 13
    mother bear in *Popcorn* 67
    Orson Abbott 12
    Peter Rabbit 13
    Rabbit in *Mr. Gumpy's Outing* 65
    Rabbit in *Who's in Rabbit's House?* 12
    White Rabbit 13
    Wilbur 13
Raggedy Ann and Andy 23 (illus)
rain in *Bringing the Rain to Kapiti Plain* 62
Ralph 81
Ramona 81–82
rat in *The Bionic Bunny Show* 13
redbird in *The Little Rabbit Who Wanted Red Wings* 12–13
Reggie in *Ira Sleeps Over* 62
reptile and amphibian, *see* boa constrictor; crocodile; dinosaur; frog; iguana; python; tortoise; turtle
Rhino in *My Father's Dragon* 74
rhinos in *Jumanji* 80
Robert in *Operation: Dump the Chump* 80
Robin Hood 46 (illus)
rooster in "The Bremen Town Musicians" 42
Rowena Jervis in *The Wish Giver* 120
runaway Ralph 81

Sam
    in *Sam* 67
    in *My Side of the Mountain* 82
    Sam-I-Am 129 (illus)
Scarecrow in *The Wizard of Oz* 73
school age characters (high school characters marked with asterisk)
    Alexander and the Terrible, Horrible, No Good, Very Bad Day (Alexander and brothers) 48

Alice's Adventures in Wonderland (Alice) 70
Ask Mr. Bear (Danny) 111
"Baa, baa, Black Sheep" (boy) 38
Bea and Mr. Jones (Bea) 53–54
Beezus and Ramona (Beezus) 71
Benji in Business (Benji and Jason) 71
Blackboard Bear books (Anthony and bully) 55
Blubber (Blubber/Linda, Robby, Wendy, and Bruce) 72
The Boy Who Turned into a TV Set (Ogden Pettibone) 79
The Cat Ate My Gymsuit (*Marcy and *Joel) 77–78
The Cat in the Hat (Sally and her brother) 55
The Champion of Merrimack County (Janet Berryfield) 79
Charlie and the Chocolate Factory (Charlie, Augustus Gloop, Veruca Salt, Violet Beauregarde, Mike Teavee) 117
Charlotte's Web (Fern) 74, 115
The Case of the Hungry Stranger (Wizard, Tubby, Skinny, paperboy, Marigold) 68
Claude the Dog (boy) 57
Corduroy (Lisa) 57
The Cricket in Times Square (Mario) 73
The Cut-Ups (Spud Jenkins and Joe Turner) 68
The Cybil War (Cybil, Simon, and Tony) 73
Danny and the Dinosaur (Danny and children) 58
Dear Mr. Henshaw (Leigh Botts) 77
Ellen Tebbits (Ellen and Austine) 74
The Fourth Grade Celebrity (Casey Valentine) 72
Freckle Juice (Andrew, Sharon, and Nicky) 70
The Ghost with the Halloween Hiccups (Laura and Bert) 10
"Goldilocks" (Goldilocks) 44
The Great Brain Reforms (Tom, Jimmy, and Danny) 82
Grinny (Timmy and Beth) 75
The Gunniwolf (Little Girl) 63–64
The Happy Lion (François) 61
Harold and the Purple Crayon (Harold) 61
Harry the Dirty Dog (children) 61
Henry Huggins (Henry, Scooter and gang) 7, 69
How to Eat Fried Worms (Billy, Alan, Joe, Tom) 71
The Indian in the Cupboard (Omri) 79–80
Ira Sleeps Over (Ira, Reggie, Ira's sister) 62
"Jack and Jill" (Jack and Jill) 40
"Jack and the Beanstalk" (Jack) 44
"Jack Be Nimble" (Jack) 40
James and the Giant Peach (James) 75–76
Jelly Belly (Ned/Nat, Richard) 76
Jumanji (Peter and Judy) 80
Jump, Frog, Jump (boys) 59
Left-Handed Shortstop (Walter Moles and Casey Valentine) 72
Lentil (Lentil) 63
The Lion, the Witch, and the Wardrobe (Peter, Susan, Edmund, and Lucy) 70–71
Little Bear Marches in the St. Patrick's Day Parade (children) 63
Little House in the Big Woods (Laura and Mary) 77
The Little Leftover Witch (Felina and Lucinda) 12
"Mary Had a Little Lamb" (Mary) 40
Mrs. Piggle-Wiggle (Patsy) 78
The Mitten ("my Grandfather") 61
Mitzi and the Elephants (Mitzi) 78
The Mouse and the Motorcycle (Keith) 81
My Father's Dragon (Elmer) 74
My Side of the Mountain (*Sam Gribley) 82
Nate the Great (Nate, Annie, and Harry) 65–66
Nothing's Fair in Fifth Grade (Elsie Edwards and the slumber party gang) 74
Old Black Witch (Nicky) 11

Character Name/Character Type Index

"The Old Woman Who Lived in a Shoe" (children) 41
Operation: Dump the Chump (Oscar and Robert Winkle) 80
Otis Spofford (Otis) 80
The Outsiders (*Pony Boy, *the Greasers, *Cherry, and *the "Socs") 81
Pippi Longstocking (Pippi, Tommy, and Annika) 80
The Pistachio Prescription (*Cassie Stephens and *Vicki) 72
The Princess and Froggie (the Princess) 60
Pumpernickle Tickle and Mean Green Cheese (Benjamin) 54
Ramona Quimby, Age 8 (Ramona, Yard Ape, and Marsha) 81
Ramona the Pest (Ramona and Howie) 81
The Secret Life of the Underwear Champ (Larry and Suzanne) 77
Soup and Me (Soup, Rob, Janice Riker, and schoolmates) 82, 119
The Stupids Have a Ball (Buster and Petunia) 112
Summer of the Monkeys (Jay Berry and Daisy) 76
Superfudge (Fudgie, Peter, and Alex Santo) 9
Tales of a Fourth Grade Nothing (Peter Hatcher, Sheila, and Jimmy) 115
Winnie-the-Pooh (Christopher Robin) 73, 83
The Wish Giver (*Adam Fiske, *Rowena Jervis, Polly Kemp, Agatha, Eunice, Leland, Lenora) 120–121
The Wizard of Oz (Dorothy) 73
the seven dwarves 46
Sharon in *Freckle Juice* 70
sheep
    in *Ask Mr. Bear* 111
    in "Baa, Baa, Black Sheep" 38
    in "Little Bo Peep" 40
    Sheep in *Mr. Gumpy's Outing* 65
Silkworm in *James and the Giant Peach* 75–76
skeletons 20 (illus), 49 (photos), 67
skunks in *A Kiss for Little Bear* 63
snake in *Jump, Frog, Jump* 59
snake, *see* boa constrictor; python
Sneetch 67
Snow White 43 (photo), 46
the "Socs" in *The Outsiders* 81
Soup 15, 82, 119
Sparrow in *Little Bear's Thanksgiving* 63
spider
    Charlotte 15 (photo), 16 (illus), 115
    in "I Know an Old Lady" 66
    in "Little Miss Muffet" 40
    Spider in *James and the Giant Peach* 75–76
spoon in "Hey, Diddle, Diddle" 38
Squeaky in *Little Bear* titles 63
squirrel
    grey (Mr. Bushy Tail in *The Little Rabbit Who Wanted Red Wings*) 12–13
    Squirrel in *Big Bear to the Rescue* 55
    Squirrel in *Little Bear's Thanksgiving* 63
    wanted by Veruca Salt in *Charlie and the Chocolate Factory* 117
Stew Meat in *The Wish Giver* 120–121
stream in *One Fine Day* 59
Strega Nona 50 (photo), 54–55
the Stupids 12, 112
the sun in *Why Mosquitoes Buzz in People's Ears* 114
Sun in *The North Wind and the Sun* 47

tailor in *The Bed Just So* 67–68
Taran in *The Black Cauldron* 120
teachers, *see* adult characters: *The Cat Ate My Gymsuit, Freckle Juice, Henry Huggins, Miss Nelson Is Missing, Sideways Stories from Wayside School, Soup and Me*
Thaddeus Blinn in *The Wish Giver* 120–121

Thing One and Thing Two 55
Three Billy Goats Gruff 46
Three Little Kittens 41
The Three Little Pigs 43 (photo), 46
Tiger in *My Father's Dragon* 74
Tigger 84 (photo)
Tin Woodman in *The Wizard of Oz* 73, 84 (photo)
Tom in *The Great Brain* titles 82
Tommy Pumpkinhead 63
Tortoise in *The Hare and the Tortoise* 44
turtle
    Dribble in *Tales of a Fourth Grade Nothing* 75
    in *Jump, Frog, Jump* 59
    Tortoise 44

Uncle Ubb 68
the underwear champ 77

the very hungry caterpillar 18 (illus), 68

wasp in *The Giant Jam Sandwich* 8
watermelon slice 27 (illus), 68
White Rabbit 13
White Witch in *The Lion, the Witch, and the Wardrobe* 70–71
Whos in *Horton Hears a Who* 61–62
wicked *oni* in *The Funny Little Woman* 60
Wilbur
    in *The Bionic Bunny* 13
    in *Charlotte's Web* 115, 116
the wild baby 68
the wild things 1 (photo), 64
Wind in *The North Wind and the Sun* 47 (illus)
Winnie-the-Pooh 73–74, 83
witch
    Betty in *Popcorn* 66–67
    Blue-Nosed Witch, Grande Madame, Minnie Max, and Josephine 12
    Dorrie 11
    Humbug Witch 11
    in Hansel and Gretel 12
    little leftover witch 12
    Old Black Witch 11
    Ramona 11
Wizard 68
The Wizard of Oz 73
wolf
    in "Little Red Riding Hood" 45
    in "The Three Little Pigs" 43 (photo), 46, 114
    in *The Wild Baby* 68
    Kapu in *Julie of the Wolves* 76
    Max in his wolf suit 64
woodcutter in "The Three Wishes" 47
woodman
    in *The Wizard of Oz* 73, 84 (photo)
    in "Little Red Riding Hood" 45

zebra in *Mitzi and the Elephants* 78

McFarlin Library
WITHDRAWN